Essex in t

Series Editor: Clive Leatherdale

Ross Gardner

DESERT ISLAND BOOKS

First published in 2007
by
DESERT ISLAND BOOKS LIMITED
7 Clarence Road, Southend-on-Sea, Essex SS1 1AN
United Kingdom
www.desertislandbooks.com

British Library Cataloguing-in-Publication Data
A catalogue record for this book is available from the British Library

ISBN 978-1-905328-26-0

Printed in Great Britain
by
4edge Ltd, Hockley. www.4edge.co.uk

Photographs courtesy of Christopher Gardner and Ross Gardner

Contents

		PAGE
	AUTHOR'S NOTE	4
1	DISCOVERING THE HIDDEN PLACES	5
2	THE ANCIENT WOODLANDS OF ESSEX: REMNANTS OF A HISTORIC LANDSCAPE	11
3	THE ESSEX COAST AND ESTUARIES: THE LAST WILDERNESS	36
4	WILDFLOWER GRASSLANDS AND HEATHER HEATHS: JEWELS OF THE ESSEX COUNTRYSIDE	79
5	ESSEX'S UNSUNG WETLANDS	100
6	NATURE THE OPPORTUNIST	126
	BIBLIOGRAPHY	138
	LIST OF SPECIES MENTIONED IN THE TEXT	140

Author's Note

This book is dedicated to the memory of Dennis Barrett,
a very dear friend.

Note on Measurements

Measurements in this book are given throughout in metric units:

One kilometre is equal to approximately 0.6 of a mile.

One hectare is 10,000 square metres, that is an enclosure measuring 100 metres in length and 100 metres in breadth. By way of comparision, a football pitch is usually around 100 metres long, by 70 metres wide.

One hectare also equals 2.471 acres, one acre being 4,840 square yards, approximately two thirds the size of a football pitch.

CHAPTER ONE

Discovering the Hidden Places

A picture. The fiery orange evening sun, low and heavy in the sky as it sinks towards the horizon of a yawning estuarine landscape. The gulls scattered along the shoreline mew their contentment, clean white plumage exchanged for darkened silhouette as they wheel up against the brooding evening sky. The sound of piping *redshank* and *oystercatcher* pierce the hushed ambience, their calls adding a dash of clarity to the pastel scene, a clear edge to the fading light and the merging shades of hazy purple, soft orange and dusky grey. As the sun melts into the tranquil waters the relentless tide laps patiently on the ebb, seemingly fatigued by another innumerable day locked in conflict with the solid but ultimately fragile estuary banks. Gathering itself for the next day's assault, its waters are placid and reflective; smooth but for the gentle ripple of the surface.

The description of a remote sea loch in the lonely reaches of Northwest Scotland? No. Rather an impression of the beautiful, wonderfully convoluted Essex coastline. To read such a dramatic account of anywhere in this county, folk might be forgiven for assuming that such superlatives are merely the rose-tinted bespectacled thoughts of some dyed-in-the-wool Essex boy, fed up with constant maligning of his home county by people who probably don't know what they are talking about anyway.

To some extent they would be right. On occasion the claim is made that Essex is flat – an assertion that must be vehemently, if perhaps a little melodramatically refuted. Okay, so Essex doesn't possess the awesomely rugged coastlines of the Southwest or the grandeur of the Scottish Highlands, but then few places do. But to take to the bicycle around the hills of Danbury, for example, would nevertheless render most of us somewhat short of breath. And while we catch said breath, we may well do it as we enjoy distant views, on a clear day extending as far as the North Downs in Kent, surrounded by orchids and rolling woodland.

So often Essex is dismissed like this – a flat boring county, a destination for counter-urbanising Londoners, blighted by overspilling development of the city and certainly not somewhere that is rich in wild beauty. While we cannot find any true wilderness in this admittedly highly populated county of ours, we can still seek out those special places; places where we can become lost in our private thoughts, surrounded by the purity of unsullied nature.

While any far-reaching vista will invariably be interrupted by the significant presence of human existence, this merely serves to accentuate the surroundings from which we make such observations. The sprawling expanse of the wild lands still found in other less-peopled corners of the country are long gone from Essex, but the fragments that survive, although lacking in measurable terms, can provide us with a depth of experience every bit as fulfilling.

This is scarcely better illustrated than when sitting among the scrubby grasslands of the Benfleet Downs and gazing out across the Thames floodplain, a view that takes in the mass of crammed housing on Canvey Island. Knowing of the glorious windy expanse of the Sheppey marshlands around Elmley and Shell Ness across the river in North Kent, a sense of what could have been – had the urban sprawl not consumed so much of the area – may begin to creep in. Had the Essex shore of the Thames Estuary been left to the lapping estuary waters, then the view would be one of empty marshland, the domain of nesting *lapwing* and *skylark* and the vast congregations of wintering wildfowl that still occur across the way. While part of me would wish for that boundless horizon, I sit and compare the incongruous spread of development in the distance to my more agreeable surroundings and it becomes evident that the intrusion of the former enhances the potency of the latter. It reminds me that where I am at that time is a good place to be, that wild Essex still survives even in the most highly developed reaches of the county. We cannot, of course, simply depopulate these places and besides, is it not from this urban environment and our suburban retreats that most of us find ourselves able to enjoy this wilder side.

In the greener parts of Essex, where the human population is thinner on the ground, the blandness of concrete is so often replaced with the sterility of intensive farming, where modern agriculture has left little room for wildlife to thrive. Strange as it seems, some of these arable deserts – in spite of their greenness – can often be more bereft of life than our townscapes, where the rows of suburban gardens may, with some irony, offer greater respite.

Here the often-used analogy of desert and verdant oasis rings especially true. Unlike in the town, the farming landscape might facilitate further reaching views. We can scan across the vast prairie style fields, shorn of their copses and hedgerows and wonder why such expansive green areas can seem so sparsely populated by wild plants and animals. Usually only those species tenacious enough to stomach the marginal existence left possible by the squeeze of modern agriculture can prevail. With our view uninterrupted we might espy the deeper green of a wood, far off on the horizon. On reaching our oasis we are enveloped by the comfortable, leafy surroundings and made starkly aware of the comparatively barren nature of the surrounding area. But as in the towns, the sense of life, though mostly unseen among branches overhead, is felt no less acutely.

Across the county we can find such opportunities. Although much developed, we may find ancient woods, wild coastlands and restful rivers. In pockets there still survives *ling* and *gorse*-clad heathlands, flower meadows and marshy floodplains. And there are times when we may stumble upon a richness of wildlife when we least expect it. To use a well-coined phrase, Essex is a county of hidden places, where its popular images do it scant justice. A traveller whose impression of the county is that of the crowded, over-developed south would know little of the picturesque and peaceful countryside that resides around the banks of the River Stour and its estuary. Even within the bustle of south Essex, the sense of seclusion felt in the leafy environs of Pound Wood – a feeling that belies its proximity to the busy A127 and numerous human dwellings – is far enough removed to remain largely unknown. And in the often vast and hedgeless farmlands, the life that surrounds that peaceful stretch of the Chelmer and Blackwater Navigation as it flows lazily towards the coast will, from the car window, often remain overlooked.

But this is not to say that our natural treasures are inaccessible and beyond our reach. As such places as Pound Wood and the Hadleigh and Benfleet Downs suggest, there are many gems to be unearthed and there can be few, if any, who would not find similar pleasures on their own doorstep. Sure enough, not everyone will have, within a five or ten minute walk, the green swathes that those places mentioned above help to comprise, but there will always be that overgrown corner in the town park, fishing lake or village pond that provides space enough for an often surprising diversity of wildlife.

A resident for several years in Chelmsford, I was constantly delighted by the unlikely charms of Central Park, located well within the town on the very fringes of the centre itself. On the park lake, within clear earshot of the urban bustle and flanked by the impressive viaduct and its rumbling trains, *great crested grebes* bred annually, along with more readily anticipated townies like *Canada geese* and *mallards*. An evening visit could be rewarded by the sight of *noctule bats*, their high, level flight punctuated by sudden spiralling dives in pursuit of prey. Meandering through the park, the River Can also had its nocturnal winged inhabitants in the shape of *Daubenton's bats*, often seen skimming the river water for unseen insects.

By day, the riverbanks sparkled with the shimmering blue presence of *banded demoiselles*, damselflies whose iridescent splendour would be ignited in the spring sunshine.

Every town, every stretch of urban sprawl has this natural edge, however much obscured, not least the two-and-a-half-thousand hectares of Epping Forest on the northeastern boundary of London and the wetlands and grasslands of the Dagenham Chase, deep in the heart of metropolitan Essex. Alight from the train at Colchester North and you are just a few minutes walk from the grassy floodplain of the River Colne; look beyond the picnickers and dog walkers at Southend's Priory Park and you might find *grey wagtails* along Prittle Brook or *flycatchers* on passage, and on the fringes of Harlow New Town you can look out onto ancient woodland complete with *fallow deer* and woodland orchids.

At this interface of town and country our imagination is captured. With a whetted appetite we may begin to ponder what lays further afield. We might become aware of the gaps within our knowledge of the local area. Public footpaths, whose finger posts we drive past every day, which only seem to pass through an uninspiring arable landscape, may just be the one that leads the inquisitive walker into an unexpected wildlife haven. For years we may have been unaware of that old pond hidden away from our more routine movements, perhaps a former watering hole for farm animals, now a haven for aquatic plants and dragonflies: or that fragment of undeveloped grassland, still adorned with wildflowers, attended by clouds of dancing butterflies and filled with the hum of singing grasshoppers.

Armed with a good map and an inquisitive mind we have all the tools we need to discover, or indeed rediscover, the Essex countryside. Much of our most valued wildlife habitat has been secured as nature reserves. The Essex Wildlife Trust owns and/or manages in excess of ninety properties, in addition to those owned by the National Trust, English Nature and the county and local authorities. Such has been the extent of degradation of the natural places of Essex, as indeed elsewhere in Britain, that prime areas are spread all too thinly, but through our Rights of Way we are able to fill in some of the gaps and bring together those areas that remain as wildlife havens.

Along hedged footpaths and leafy bridleways we may, to some extent, knit together a pattern of wild Essex, albeit at times somewhat tenuously. In Hockley Woods we find a splendid area of ancient woodland, well served itself by trails within. But radiating from it are footpaths that lead south across surrounding farmland taking in a clutch of other smaller woods. And to the north, with just the inconvenience of a few hundred metres of roadside walking, a half a dozen more are connected via public footpaths – not to mention other outlying areas of woodland hardly any further afield. Hockley Woods is, in itself, an area of much fascination and one of our finest areas of ancient woodland, but by placing it into a wider context, as part of the local landscape, this interest is enhanced. On our visit to Hockley we are no longer restricted to the eponymous wood, but our wanderings may take us further, allowing us to explore more fully a corner of the countryside hitherto unknown, or at least under-appreciated, concealed by the suburbia that impinges so heavily from beyond.

Even among the peace and quiet of the sparsely populated rural quarters of Essex where the yearning for open space is far less acutely evident, we are still able to further enrich our experience, even without the frustrations of urban life to which we can make our comparisons. The flurry of life amid the agricultural blandness is as noticeable as it is in the centre of a busy town. While the isolated bastions of wildlife habitat provoke a sense of defiance, it is where the land gives way to the coast that we really begin to experience the wilder reaches of our county.

It is along the banks of yawning estuaries and through endless views over windswept marshes that we are given a taste of wilderness. Far from the busy seafront of the Thames (which incidentally still provides some of the best winter bird watching in Essex), the saltmarsh and grazing marshes of the Blackwater Estuary provide a rugged and timeless setting, as calming and peaceful in the summertime as anyone could want, yet so exposed and wonderfully uncompromising amid the British winter.

Along the uncharacteristically straight edge (given the more erratic profile of much of the Essex coastline) of the Dengie Peninsula is a coastal expanse as remote as you might find anywhere else, certainly over the greater part of Eastern England. And in the most northeasterly reaches of the county lies the wonderfully picturesque and tranquil estuary of the River Stour, a seamless continuation of the beautiful and famous Dedham Vale further inland.

From the local park to the gaping sweep of the coast, the wild plants and animals that survive in Essex paint a fascinating and, perhaps to some, surprising picture: a mosaic rich in substance and experience, despite the growing pressures of a demanding human population. Wherever we are we can experience the pleasures of living side by side with nature. There will always be that spot, one's local patch that nine times out of ten will be overlooked by the casual or infrequent visitor to a town or village and if noticed only rarely given a second thought. But the local will over time compose a detailed and personal portrait of an essentially unknown area of wildlife habitat. How many, for instance, know that included in the list of thirty-plus birds that are to be found around the ancient castle earthworks of Rayleigh Mount, are such locally uncommon species as *grey wagtail* and *pied flycatcher?*

In some places nature thrives in abundance, in others it lives a frontier existence. But from the spectacle of vast flocks of wading birds wheeling over some lonely marsh and the magical sight of wild deer to the unlikely sight of bats and breeding water birds in the middle of town, the rewards and the thrills they trigger are consistently the same.

CHAPTER TWO

The Ancient Woodlands of Essex: Remnants of a Historic Landscape

FROM PAST TO PRESENT

The wooded landscape of Essex has, in common with the rest of the British Isles, experienced much change over the millennia. Not only has the area of woodland dramatically decreased, the nature of the woodland itself has been altered by centuries of human influence.

As the last Ice Age came to an end, some 12,000 years ago, the retreating ice sheets allowed species that had been forced south by the cooling climate to reclaim their former grounds. By 9500 BP (before present) late glacial species, such as *dwarf birch* and *willow* were present in Essex, later on with *pine*, *hazel* and *elm*. Over the following 4,000 years, under a stable and temperate climate, the wildwood developed, from the post-glacial scrub into something that we might today have found more familiar. By 5500 BP wildwood covered the county, comprising *oak, lime, hazel and elm*.

But change was imminent. As the human, hunter-gatherer inhabitants of Britain began to learn the methods and advantages of a more sedentary existence, so began the reshaping of the landscape. By 5000 BP early Essex farmers were clearing woodland to make way for crop cultivation and livestock grazing. Come the Iron Age (2500 BP), as much as half of the wildwood in Britain may have already been cleared.

The trend of wildwood deforestation had been initiated and was set to persist, albeit inconsistently throughout the coming centuries. The Romans continued the woodland clearances apace, in Essex on a large scale, perhaps involving a third of the woodland remaining in the county. This wasn't solely for the acquisition of timber for building and to clear land for agriculture, as the Romans brought with them new technologies and ideas, such as the manufacture of glass and brick, all requiring fuel to drive the production processes.

There was little change on the woodland landscape during the succeeding Saxon period, but a near doubling of the population of medieval England between the 11th and 14th centuries resulted in a further retraction of wooded land. Over the years that followed, British woodland enjoyed a period of respite. As the iron industry began to flourish, the importance of a sustainable method of woodland management, i.e. coppicing, was favoured to the felling of mature trees in order to ensure a steady supply of wood for charcoal to fuel the smelting processes. It was not until the 19th century and the increased timber demands of the two world wars that further significant clearances were carried out.

Even through periods of stability, when significant changes in area were absent, the fabric of the woodland itself was being altered as humans continued to exploit it for the resources that they offered. It is this long history of human intervention and management that was to change the wildwood forever. The earliest evidence of woodland management in Britain is provided by ancient Neolithic trackways (c5000 BP) that were built using small trees and poles acquired from coppiced woodland. It is possible that in Essex some woodland management was being undertaken by at least 2,500 years ago.

Although very different from the ancestral wildwood, our woodlands today still generate a mystical and timeless atmosphere that, it is tempting to think, would have pervaded such places in the past. One may be forgiven for feeling a sense of mourning for the loss of the wildwood as we may imagine it was and for regarding its metamorphosis into 'modern' woodland in a negative light. But as the wildwood changed, so too did the floral and faunal communities that thrived within. It is the devastating retraction of our wooded land that should be grieved for, the denial of the vast and presumably breathtaking tracts of wooded country of the past.

But let this not detract from what remains. Although the wildwood is long gone, some parts of the countryside have maintained a cover of trees without interruption, still harbouring the diverse wildlife communities that recall their true origins. In other places woodland has regenerated following earlier clearances, over the centuries regaining the richness of the ancestral landscape. In 'official' terms, an ancient wood is one that dates from before 1600. That which has developed more recently is referred to as secondary woodland.

Woodland in the modern environment has a singularly enveloping effect that other places may scarcely match, a sensation that is ironically heightened by the isolation and encapsulation of our woods. Many of those in Essex now exist in juxtaposition with the sterile urban or agricultural landscapes that predominate, serving to make more profound the almost tangible sensation of leaving the contrived and passing into environs of natural design. From beneath the towering trunks and their copious foliage there is an almost corporeal sense of being consumed by the place, of being removed from the world beyond the woodland edge. While the summer sun bakes the ground outside the woods, from beneath the tree canopy one can enjoy the kaleidoscopic play of light through the leaves from the cool woodland floor, the dappled rays creating a collage of green shades of seemingly infinite variety; an autumn wind howls unhindered across the adjacent open land, but the weathered boughs of old battle-hardened trees roar their defiance, bearing the brunt to the benefit of those below.

Coppicing has been the principal method of woodland management, certainly since at least the early medieval times (c11th century) and has played a key role in shaping the woodlands of today. It is a sustainable method of harvesting wood whilst ensuring a continuously regenerating crop each year. During the coppice rotation of anything between five and twenty years, a section of a wood would be cut each year, with the exception of a number of mature standards (timber trees), safe in the knowledge that the stumps would sprout back and eventually grow into multi-stemmed stools to form the underwood. A different area would be cut each year leaving the underwood of previously coppiced areas to regenerate. The timber trees would have been used for building and the underwood would have yielded rods and poles for fencing and tool making and wood for logs and charcoal.

It was not until the late 19th century that coppicing went into decline, a demise that lasted into the middle of the 20th century. The produce derived from coppicing was becoming increasingly undesirable. With the advent of coal and coke fuel, the coppiced woods became less and less important for the firewood that they could provide, while an increasing shift towards plantation forestry signalled a further death knell for this traditional practice.

There has been something of a recent revival in traditional woodland management and commercially managed coppice can be found in various parts of the county. It is also a key aspect of wildlife management and it is perhaps in this guise that most of us will be familiar with in Essex. Conservation bodies, such as the Essex Wildlife Trust and the National Trust, are often keen to reinstate traditional coppice management, especially into woods where a long history of coppicing is known.

Through each phase of the coppice rotation distinct ecological niches are created. As human intervention gradually altered the woodland structure, plants and animals adapted to these changes. Where the wood is cleared a greater variety of flora and fauna can thrive, making the most of the sunny, open conditions. As the coppice regenerates, the resulting thickets offer nesting opportunities for skulking birds, maybe *nightingale* or *blackcap*. Thus, a visit to a coppiced wood, when a heavy hand has been resisted, is a varied experience. The coppice rotation against a backdrop of high forest (uncoppiced woodland left to its own devices), dominated by majestic towering standards sheltering the airy shrub layer below, creates an aesthetic and stimulating environment, where an eclectic mix of woodland plants and animals means we might always be surprised by something.

The large, open clearings that result add another dimension to woodland life. During late spring the unimpeded rays of the sun brings forth a flush of growth on the ground, with grasses like *sweet vernal grass* or the dense green tussocks of *tufted hair grass*, the purple blooms of *willowherbs* or the little yellow trumpets of *cow-wheat*. Embraced by older coppice or mature woodland, the buzz of life here seems more intense, more concentrated. Those animals unable to tolerate the cooler, shaded surrounds add extra vibrancy to the woodland scene. Butterflies abound, not just the *speckled wood*, a true woodland stalwart, but also *comma, brimstone* and others. *Bush crickets* 'sing' their contentment from their hidden perches, while the myriad nameless other creatures fill the place with their relentless activity.

Many Essex woods, however, have long ago ceased to be managed, and by following the maze of public footpaths that snake across the county this 'neglected' woodland can often be found. Neglected because these are woods that have not been managed for several decades, often more. But the multi-stemmed trunks of long untouched coppice stools betray a history of human intervention, where old *sweet chestnut* boughs have attained a girth resembling that of the standards alongside which they grow. The tree canopy, long since closed overhead, casts a heavy shade over the ground and although such woods may not match the diversity of wildlife found in managed woodland (although some woods, such as Marylands Wood in Hockley, harbour a rich flora, in spite of many years of non-intervention), their presence in the countryside is no less valuable.

Here we see nature beginning to reassert itself in the absence of human interference as the old coppice reverts unwaveringly towards high forest. Shade-tolerant plants like *broad-leaved helleborine* and *enchanter's night-shade* enjoy the freedom of a more spacious woodland floor, but only along the woodland edges or naturally occurring clearings do we find the plants and animals recognisable of the open coppice. Shafts of glaring sunlight pour down only through the apertures in the canopy left by aged fallen trees to create a bold contrast with the darker hues of the shaded surrounds. Energised, the woodland floor explodes into life. From the homogenous ground cover of *bramble* and *honeysuckle* erupts an array of other species, perhaps *foxglove* or *stitchwort*.

These woods show how rapidly the doings of humans are left behind but at the same time leaving a lasting signature of our presence. Not only do the signs of coppicing persist, but also the earth banks, which once demarcated the boundaries of the woods or ownership within them, may indicate a more distant history. These can sometimes date back well into the medieval times, perhaps even earlier.

Our woods convey an impression of history, of quiet contemplation. It takes a long time for a wood to become a wood and it is almost as if in doing so, they have absorbed something of the past into their great fissured boughs and twisted old coppice stools. There is a solidity and permanence associated with ancient woodland. It has been much pondered that if we were able to commune with the trees, what could they tell us? If their stories could be passed on from generation to generation, as we have acquired knowledge of our ancestors, what then could we learn from the centuries-old *oaks* that still reside over our woodlands today?

In parts of Essex we are presented with a living snapshot of this sense of history, an indication of the historical importance of our wooded landscape. In medieval times the whole county comprised the royal Forest of Essex, where the King held the hunting rights of the deer and wild boar that roamed within. Royal forests were typically rather open in nature, indeed some 'forests' were barely wooded at all, the cover of trees often dissected by wide chases that connected open plains. It is at Hatfield Forest that one of the finest examples of medieval royal forest in the country, or perhaps even Europe, has been preserved. It is a compartmented forest. Areas of woodland were coppiced and fenced off to protect the new growth from browsing deer or livestock – the plains providing accessible areas.

Where the woodland was not compartmented, trees were pollarded. This is effectively a method of coppicing by taking the wood from between two to four-and-a-half metres off the ground atop a trunk, or bolling. This left the new growth to develop beyond the reach of foraging animals. On a still crisp January morning, a heavy frost crunching beneath your feet and the presence of each exhaled breath betrayed by the cold winter air; ribbons of mist drifting low and wraith-like across the lake and dense clumps of evergreen *mistletoe* hanging conspicuously from the boughs of bare winter trees, it is not difficult to picture yourself standing amid a genuine medieval scene.

Although scarcely as well preserved, we find elsewhere echoes of an historic wooded Essex. At Epping Forest, the airy canopies of great *beech* trees, their smooth trunks furrowed by the passage of time, create an appropriately timeless atmosphere. Unlike Hatfield Forest, Epping was originally an uncompartmented forest where deer and livestock could once roam freely. Here, therefore, we find many pollarded trees. When regularly cut, the commoners would have grazed their livestock on the 'wood-pasture' that flourished beneath. Epping has suffered through the neglect of the past. Where traditional management methods have abated, the forest has been deprived of its pastures and its heathy glades left to become overgrown. But the old ways are now being reinstated, so as to revisit the Forest of old and enhance the magical ambience that the place undoubtedly still delivers.

At Hatfield and Epping it is easy to appreciate how the woodland captures the imagination and can so easily distract one to thoughts of the ancient, spreading forests, as – also it should be added – do those discrete little pockets of woodland, standing bravely in the face of advancing concrete and modern agriculture. Many of the large mammals that once dwelt within these Essex woods of old have long since gone, but we still have the chance, particularly in the north of the county, of that thrilling glimpse of a *fallow deer* buck, looking up with a start as he hears your approach, displaying his impressive palmate antlers.

His ancestors in centuries past would have been alert to the huntsman of which he was their chosen quarry. During those first moments on sighting you, his heart would still pound as it would have back then. He briefly fixes your gaze and for just a moment the boundaries are lost; who is the observer and who is the observed? Then he succumbs to his instinct and disappears into the cover of the understorey, procuring a fleeting image of the wildwood, a small piece of how life was in that verdant, boundless forest. The wood is an intimate place where such moments as these can strike a chord within, instigating a flicker of recognition where everything fits: the observer, the observed and their shared environment existing for that moment in total unity.

We have a strong affinity with our woodlands, arguably more so than anywhere else. The forestlands of Britain in the days of yore are the stuff of legend, recalling the fabled adventures of the great King Arthur and the noble thief Robin Hood. Our woods of today perhaps capture something of the romanticism of the folklore so firmly entrenched within the ancient landscape of our past. But maybe the ties run more deeply. Deciduous woodland is the climax community of the greater part of Britain and virtually the whole of Essex; that state of equilibrium that nature must unerringly strive towards. Maybe deep within our subconscious, where resides that primal, instinctive facet of our consciousness, a kind of empathy is achieved with this most 'natural' of habitats, facilitating that sense of closeness with the wooded environment.

With this in mind, it appears ever more absurd that we have in the past endeavoured to relieve ourselves so drastically of our indigenous natural heritage. While it is true that most of the originally wooded land in Britain was deforested many centuries ago, long before the notion of conservation was ever perceived, it is not as if, in more recent times, we have cherished what remained.

Much of Essex has been given over to development (most notably in the south) and the intensive cultivation of the fertile soils. Extensive tracts of ancient woodland are therefore few and far between. But on the other hand, we can count ourselves lucky. Other eastern counties, such as Cambridgeshire and Norfolk, are among the least wooded in Britain. In Essex most of us are fortunate enough to live at least reasonably close to significant areas of woodland. Although mere fragments of what they once were, they are a valuable wildlife resource and remain to stimulate and inspire.

WOODLAND WILDLIFE: THE MOST DIVERSE IN BRITAIN

The most diverse and varied assemblages of flora and fauna in the Britain are found in ancient woodland. Over the thousands of years since the dawning of the ancestral forest the woodland ecosystem has come to encompass the lives and interactions of many and various plants and animals. But so often these can go unnoticed by the casual observer who may at first not see beyond the ubiquitous spread of common plants like *wood melick, honeysuckle and bramble,* and the familiar faces of *blackbirds, robins* and squirrels. The initial impression of woodland life will often belie richness within.

The flux of life in the wood is a most dynamic one. It is a place where the seasons of the year come and go with marked contrast. As they arrive and depart, so we are made aware of the variety of life that dwells within the woodland habitat, each year punctuated by the predictable but always welcomed reappearance of old friends. How grateful we are for the springtime cacophony of birdsong and the fresh, eager green of the early shoots of *hawthorn* and *hornbeam.* We look ahead to the first flowers of spring – often the refreshing white blooms of *wood anemone,* or the March return of the *chiff chaff,* stridently announcing his arrival with that bright and cheerful song. The pace slows for the balmy days of summer, when the frenetic activity of nesting and fledgling birds gives way to the incessant hum of tireless woodland insects. Then there is the blaze of autumn colour, with the burnished colours of changing leaves. Troops of mushrooms – the likes of the concave capped *milkcaps,* colourful robust *russula* and such justifiably ominous sounding species as the *death cap* and *panther cap* – issue from beneath the golden, leaf-covered carpet and tiers of *many-zoned polypore* and *sulphur tuft* smother the rotting stumps. Then follows the stark naked boughs of winter and the purposeful search for food by those that choose to remain for the duration. We might be warmed against the chill by the presence of the tiny *goldcrest*, seemingly oblivious to the cold on their ceaseless quest for unseen, miniscule insects hidden among the branches. Each season and the experiences that they offer are distinctive, but the transition between them never abrupt.

THE GREEN MOSAIC

The richness of woodland wildlife is to a great extent typified by its flora: ancient woodland will contain a particularly interesting one. Throughout the existence of these old woods a host of plants may have come to be present. Some species are only, or at least for the great majority of the time, found in such woods and are thus looked upon as indicators of ancient woodland.

With countywide distribution, *oak, ash* and *sweet chestnut* may be regarded as the mainstay of Essex woodland trees. The *small-leaved lime*-dominated woodland which was once so prevalent over much of lowland Britain is now much more scarce. In Essex it is confined largely to the north of the county, at such notable locations as Chalkney Wood near Earls Colne.

We perhaps regard the *oak* as the grand-daddy of them all and not without reason. A centuries-old English *oak* with its massive boughs and great domed crown has a presence in any landscape. Even as one of thousands of other trees within a wood, that mighty old *oak* will still stand alone. Beyond the aesthetics they are among the most ecologically productive of all British plants. Rivalled only by the *willows*, the *oak* is known to support more than six hundred different species of invertebrate.

The *sweet chestnut* is unique, in that it is the only tree mentioned here that is not a true native of the British Isles, but all the same, chestnut woodland can be found all over Essex. This Southern European species was brought to our shores during the Roman occupation, an excellent tree for timber and its nuts an important source of food. *Sweet chestnut* has since become something of an honorary native. They are undoubtedly a part of the ancient woodland flora of Essex. At woods like Norsey and Pound, massive old coppice stools, some of them two-and-a-half metres across, are testament to many years of woodsmanship and the presence of the trees for a considerable length of time. It is a handsome enough tree, as these spectacular monuments bear out, but woods dominated by *chestnut*, although fine places to spend time do seem to lack something of the luxuriance and copiousness of indigenous woods of *oak* or *ash*.

And what of the other trees that can be found? Over many parts of Essex the *hornbeam* is an important understorey species. Its hard, dense wood means that many of those that we find today are in the form of multi-stemmed coppiced stools, their crop having been much harvested over the years. Although often overshadowed by imposing *oak* standards, and in spite of their diminutive coppiced habit, the *hornbeam* is a delightful tree. Early to flush, their virgin leaves of spring are an embodiment of the renewed vibrancy of the season. As sheets of buds break out over the spreading branches, the more austere hues of the winter woodland past are obliterated by the sudden profusion of fresh, vivid green foliage. In places, standard trees, or at least very old coppiced plants are still a prominent feature, when the contours of the smooth, fluted bark are further exaggerated with deep furrows, marvellously knarled boughs stretching out over the woodland floor. Thorndon Country Park (North) boasts some magnificent specimens, offering an uncommon opportunity to appreciate fully mature *hornbeam* standards.

There are, of course, many others that comprise the tree communities of Essex woods. *Birch* and *hazel* are widely distributed across the county, the latter often another important species of the understorey, while others such as *rowan* – surely among the most attractive of native trees – *cherry* and *crab apple* are all to be encountered. Arguably the most important tree of Essex woods is *wild service*. This is a nationally rare plant, but is a feature of many Essex woods, particularly in the southeast and may even be quite common in some, such as West Wood (Thundersley) and Hockley Woods. It is an indicator of ancient woodland. Unlike the smooth grey bark of its close relative the *rowan*, that of the *wild service* is rougher and at a glance might be overlooked among the trunks of neighbouring *oak* trees. However, like its relation, its foliage is distinctive; it does not share the pinnate, ash-like leaves of the *rowan*, having those that resemble a *maple* (but not arranged in opposite pairs about the stem like a member of the *Acer* family).

The distribution of trees will often say much about the geography and topography, where certain species will predominate under certain conditions. *Alder* is a familiar tree of the damp stream valleys in Essex woods (where *willows* may also find a favourable environment): of the two native *oaks*, *sessile* is the more dominant on poor soils. By nature's design a wood may develop a mosaic of tree communities, where subtle changes in species composition occur, perhaps even without the visitor really noticing. This principle of a mosaic of species carries over to the flora as a whole. Not only will soils and surface features play a part, but also the types of trees present and the levels of shade that they cast. Mature beech trees for example, intercept up to eighty percent of sunlight, whereas ash will allow the same amount to warm the ground below. This will have obvious consequences for anything trying to grow underneath and, needless to say, is a fundamental principle behind the resurgence of ground flora following coppicing. This is not to say that, in a qualitative sense, one woodland type is always better than another, but that they are merely different.

An exceptionally rich wood may have in excess of three hundred species of flowering plants. Even an 'average' one might still boast a three-figure total and will almost always be woods where some kind of rotational management is being undertaken. As described above, coppicing brings forth a profusion of different species into the confines of a wood. A coppice flora is a transient one, the composition of species changing as rapidly as the regeneration of the newly cut stools.

But the flora of a wood is not just about numbers. It's about the welcoming robustness of the trees, their arching canopies and their copiously adorned branches; a world in some respects as mysterious and hidden to the human visitor as the murk of the sea bed. It's about the verdant understorey, be it the lush *fern* and *sedge*-lined stream valleys or the tangle of *bramble* and *honeysuckle* where skulks those creatures that give a woodland that sense of abundant yet unseen life. By way of analogy, there may other places in Essex that might harbour more types of plant than the *beech* woods of Epping Forest, but here is to be found some of the most inspiring and majestic woodland in the county.

Essex woods can offer some of the most breathtaking wildlife spectacles in Britain. There must surely be few who can fail to be astounded by the sheets of *bluebell* that can turn a woodland floor into an ocean of flowers, infusing the air with a scent so pervading that it can almost be tasted. These are the sights and smells of the springtime wood. The great majority of woodland flowers appear early in the year, before the shade is cast by the tree canopy in full leaf. There are those who have travelled the globe and seen the natural wonders of the world that still hold the magnificent display of *bluebells* in British woods in the same high esteem. There are some *bluebell* woods, such as Blakes Wood and Norsey Wood, where this cerulean carpet stretches as far as can be seen between the boughs of the encompassing trees, interrupted only by the occasional blooms of *yellow archangel* and *red campion*, or *wood anemones* still vying for space with hoards of *bluebell*, having preceded the latter with a quantity impressive in its own right.

Blakes Wood, along with the hundred-odd hectares of the nearby Danbury Ridge Complex, is a fine area for woodland flora. The undulating terrain (in Essex terms at least) draws the walker along criss-crossing footpaths through woodland of *oak, sweet chestnut* and *hornbeam*. There are stream valleys clad with *ferns*, the banks coloured in the spring by *celandine, primrose* and *bugle*. The curious *moschatel* is so easily overlooked, with its five cryptically coloured green flowers, arranged in 'town hall clock' fashion, but once spotted will often be found growing in great quantity. *Lily-of-the-valley*, in parts, grows in such swathes as to make this plant something of a speciality of the area. Even before the flower spikes appear, gently yielding to the weight of a handful of white, bell-shaped flowers, their broad, orchid-like leaves have a beauty of their own.

Essex woodland does indeed have its orchids. Often being plants that prefer base-rich soils, and although occurring in various parts of the county, the richest orchid woods are to the northwest, where chalky boulder clay – as opposed to heavier clays that predominate over much of Essex – provides a more favourable habitat for these plants. These are plants that would seem to capture the imagination more so than other, perhaps less distinctive families. Even the unobtrusive pink and mauve flower spikes of *broad-leaved helleborine*, when inspected more closely, reveal itself to possess the exquisite blooms that one expects from a member of the orchid family. They are one of the more widespread species of orchid in Essex, gracing the shady woodlands of the south as well as the north. Some woods may boast *greater butterfly-orchid*, a beautiful plant with spikes of delicate and ornate white flowers, which are ironically known for being pollinated by nocturnal moths. The charms of the *early-purple orchid* are perhaps more obvious, their profusion of bold pink-purple flowers always a welcome find.

Other chalk-loving species are to be found in this region. The *oxlip* is arguably one of the most important. They are something of a speciality of Eastern England with its British range condensed into an area encompassing Cambridgeshire, Suffolk and northwest Essex, where this delightful *Primula* may occur in considerable local abundance. Such woods as the EWT reserves of Shadwell Wood and West Wood (Uttlesford) are of particular importance for this species, as indeed they are for other calcicolous plants like the *orchids* and *herb-paris*.

Even though it is the varied woodland habitats of managed woods that tend to harbour the greatest numbers of species, there are, needless to say, shade specialists, even beneath the shadows cast by the summer canopy in full leaf. Where the varied colours of woodland flowers are less frequent, the verdant green of ferns offer ample consolation. In a region of Britain with a climate too dry for many species, *male* and *broad-buckler fern* occur throughout Essex, thriving in the less competitive environment of the shaded woodland. And there are, of course, wildflowers to be found. *Enchanter's nightshade* will yield a sprinkling of tiny white blooms, sparkling in the dappled light of the path edge, while *broad-leaved helleborine* positively relish the deep shade.

Nevertheless, the opening of the canopy triggers a riot of growth. Warmed and revitalised by the returning heat of the sun on the soil, dormant seeds germinate, even after decades of inactivity. Plants like *foxglove* and *wood spurge* awaken to adorn the new coppice with their conspicuous presence. In places, like Pound Wood, new clearings may become inundated with *common cow-wheat* in its endeavour to cover every last bit of bare ground, its exuberant growth a reflection of its resurgence after years of inertness. Other species, whose seeds do not persist in the soil, colonise from elsewhere. Typical are the windblown seeds of the elegant *rosebay willowherb*, a true opportunist, ensuring a splash of colour in the new coppice landscape, giving rise to stands of vivid pink blooms.

If not choked by *bramble*, a grassy habitat will soon develop. Grasses such as *Yorkshire fog* and *sweet vernal grass* may be quick to take advantage, alongside more typical woodland species, like the *tufted hair-grass*, their inflorescence impressively displayed on tall, arching plumes, launching from the dense leafy tussock.

As the coppice regenerates, the recent arrivals are shaded out, with scene to be enacted elsewhere in the coppice rotation, so the cycle of woodland life perpetuates.

THE UNSEEN MYRIADS

The vegetative richness of our woods is reflected by the huge diversity of invertebrate life that thrives on this opulent floral array. Many rely on particular plants to complete their life cycles, and even those who might not have specific tastes may still exhibit preferences to certain species. Thus the rich tapestry of plant life facilitates the impressive faunal assemblages associated with ancient woodland.

The wildlife of the ancient woodland habitat is the most diverse in the country, but for most of us the lives of woodland animals are carried out beyond our sight. Aside from the much-observed birds and squirrels, a wood is a secretive place, one that purveys an overwhelming sense of the many beings that live within, but so many of which we are scarcely privy to – a fact that can frequently frustrate those keen for a view of some elusive creature, not to the point of irritation, rather an eagerness to know more, all the while reassured by their presence, whether to be seen or not.

While it is the woodland birds and the few more obvious mammals that provide the public face, as it were, of woodland fauna, the vast majority of animals present are those that will remain largely unseen, but for those who seek them out. A great many invertebrates are to be found in our woods, but few will be aware of the tiny creatures that live beneath the leaf litter, or of the beetles and woodlice that forage amidst the bark of the stumps and dead trunks, keeping a tree 'alive' even after its death.

And then there are the myriads that inhabit the still-living crowns of mature trees. Some leave clues to their presence. The small discs clustered on the underside of *oak* leaves are caused by tiny *gall wasps* (*Neuroterus quercusbaccarum*). Their eggs are laid into the leaves and on hatching cause the plant to swell and engulf the larva. Protected within, the grubs feed on the nutritious tissue of the gall. But just how many thousands of individual sawflies, aphids, flies and wasps will a single mature *oak* tree sustain? How can we even begin to guess? As the tip of the invertebrate iceberg, those creatures that we encounter are the ones that give us an insight into this mysterious world.

Ancient woodland is a habitat that teems with invertebrate life. From the dark damp world of the leaf litter, right up to the dizzying heights of the tallest trees, every niche is occupied. A single square metre of ground may harbour many thousands of *springtails*, primitive insects, scavengers of decaying plant matter and microscopic fungi beneath the leaf litter. Multitudes of small spiders hunt above the fallen leaves and leaf mulch. The *wolf spider (Pardosa lugubris)*, is often abundant, a diminutive but fearsome predator with no need for spinning a web, hunting instead with stealth and speed.

The seemingly redundant presence of rotting timber provides a crucial habitat. Peel back the bark of some rotting log and another realm is revealed. Wood-boring beetles attempt to hide in the crevices in an effort to keep out of sight. Some beetles are associated with decaying wood only in their larval stages. From an unsightly looking, plump white grub, a striking adult may develop, like the impressive yellow and black *Strangalia maculata*, a common *longhorn beetle* of Essex woods. *Centipedes* and *millipedes* flee from the sunlight, scuttling away for fear of desiccation. The former is a predator and a remarkable little creature. Without the facility of sight, the *centipede* tracks its prey (small insects, *woodlice* or even other *centipedes*) by touch, able to feel even the slightest of vibrations. Once captured, the victim is dispatched with poison claws. These deadly weapons are in fact modified legs located either side of the head.

These creatures may not capture the imagination of everyone, but through our awareness of these covert lives we are given a profile of the enormous diversity of life in the wood. The fascination that we can derive from them, if we so choose to do so, is every bit as expansive as their variety of form and complexity of interaction.

But if the appeal of some so-called 'creepy crawlies' isn't perhaps immediately obvious, there are those that instantly endear and amaze. In common with the alarming trend over much of Britain, Essex woods have lost many species of butterfly over the decades. Since the 1950s Hadleigh Great Wood, for example, has lost ten species, some that were once plentiful in the area. Our butterflies are still, nevertheless, a significant and valuable aspect of our woodland fauna. Thankfully there are those that are still to be encountered throughout the county. The *speckled wood* is frequently met, fluttering along the dappled woodland rides or rejoicing in the columns of sunlight that succeed in breaching the canopy. And that most arboreal of butterflies, the *purple hairstreak*, remains widespread, wherever there are plenty of *oak* trees on which to deposit their eggs. The adult, like their larva, also take their food from the high foliage. Only during very dry summers do they descend to take nectar from flowers at ground level, gaining their replenishment instead, from honeydew, the sweet secretion left by *aphids* that coats the leaves on even the loftiest boughs. Their penchant for the high crowns of their foodplant means that they provide something more of a challenge to spot. There are, however, few other butterflies that inhabit the treetops in any number.

Other woodland stalwarts like the *pearl-bordered fritillaries* and the magnificent *purple emperor* have long since disappeared from Essex woods, but there is another that still remains and has been enjoying a period of increase. The delightful Stour Wood, set above the picturesque estuary of the same name, is an Essex stronghold of the *white admiral*. With an upperside black, but for the white band emblazoned across its wings, this is a most handsome butterfly and a true woodland species. Ignoring the more profuse masses of the sweet-smelling *honeysuckle* that flourish in the sunlight of the ride edges, the female instead seeks out the more straggly specimens deeper into the wood on which to lay her eggs. For such a boldly patterned species it can be a rather elusive creature.

There is another jewel to be found in our woods, one that is as rare as it is exquisite. The *heath fritillary* is a most scarce butterfly in Britain. Being so closely associated with coppiced woodland, they suffered more than most through the uninterest in woodland management during the early 20th century and was subsequently shaded out of many of its traditional haunts, to the extent that its range retracted to a mere handful of sites in Kent and the Southwest. Efforts have been made to bring the *heath fritillary* back from the brink, with several reintroductions into Essex woods.

And what if they had been lost altogether? The sight of these beautiful little butterflies, skimming low across the open coppice and swathes of *common cow-wheat*, their foodplant, or seeking the sweet nectar of *bramble* blossom is one of the true delights of late spring. Intricately marked with rich chestnut brown and black chequered upperwings – the underside is a mosaic of white, orange and yellow – it is not only their scarcity that makes them special. Where the butterfly seems to have become particularly well established, namely at Hockley Woods and Hadleigh Great Wood, they can often appear so numerous as to make a mockery of their perilous status.

For every butterfly we see in the woods there will be many different species of moth. All belonging to the same order, the *Lepidoptera*, we find no scientific distinction between butterflies and moths, but instead a division based on physiology and behaviour; a great many – but by no means all – moths rest with their wings flat to their backs and are nocturnal. A large number of moths are associated with woodland trees and shrubs: around two hundred on *birch* and *oak* and several dozen each on the likes of *hazel, alder, apple, beech* and *hornbeam*. Nevertheless, the self-effacing behaviour of nocturnal moths means that as long as it takes to find most of the butterfly residents, one will have only scratched the surface of the moth community.

Moths reflect the resourcefulness of the *Lepidoptera*, exploiting every aspect of the woodland habitat. There are micromoths that lay their eggs into dead wood, fungi and even dead animals. The *green longhorn* is a conspicuous day-flying micromoth, frequently encountered in our woods. Metallic green wings and extraordinarily long antennae render them most distinctive. In the spring these tiny moths can be seen in swarms, hovering about some sun-drenched tree seemingly singled out from any others in the vicinity. Their larvae, however, are raised on dead leaves in the litter of the woodland floor. *Degeer's longhorn* is another colourful member of the *Adelinae* family, with a golden sheen to its wings, broken by a band of yellow. It also feeds on leaf litter, but has the further distinction of the males possessing the longest antennae of all British moths.

Of course, it is usually the living tissues of plants that are more commonly devoured and there won't be any aspect of the woodland flora left unattended. There are species that feed on mosses, and others, like the *footman moths*, which seek out *lichen* on which to lay their eggs.

But it is the higher woodland plants that support the greatest number of species. The *oak* has many devotees. The *oak hook-tip* is a widespread moth of Essex woodlands, occasionally known to break from its nocturnal routine when they may be seen flying around the upper branches in the afternoon sun. The larvae of the *green oak tortrix* feed on the buds or rolled-over leaves, sometimes with devastating defoliating effect. The diminutive green-winged adults are frequently encountered, but it is perhaps the similarly coloured caterpillars that we are more likely to meet, dangling from the branches on silken threads. Of the other species that number the *oak* among their foodplants, the pale wings of the *common white wave* are one of the easier moths to see in the gloom of the darkened wood. The butterfly-like *purple thorn*, one of a group of moths that may rest with their wings closed above their back, may take to the wing as dusk falls, at least offering a chance of detection without cause for braving the woods at night.

Birch is just as productive. Amongst the many, it is used by the *orange underwing,* an early flyer in the spring sunshine of March and April and one sure to be met with in many of the woods of Essex. Just another small brown moth, but for the flash of orange on the hindwing, glimpsed as they twist and turn their way high into the treetops; very much a herald of the season.

And while the other woodland trees, such as *beech, ash* and the numerous others, cannot match the prolificacy of the *oak* and *birch*, they add so very much to the overall richness of our woodland invertebrate fauna.

THE SONGSTERS AND THE SECRETIVE

With so much of woodland life unseen to the human eye, it is the larger animals that often provide the first clues to this hidden wealth. Despite lacking the visual spectacle of our coastal marshlands, the bird life of Essex woodland is as rich and varied as one might expect. It tends to be the larger tracts of woodland where we stand a better chance of viewing the widest range of birds, such as the forests of Writtle and Epping and also the smaller, but nonetheless extensive areas of Hockley Woods and the Danbury Ridge.

There are few better places to celebrate the coming of spring than the wood, resonating to the vocal splendour of birds, their keenness to be heard so much more intense after the quieter months that have gone before. Yet in the depths of winter the clear, loud call of the *great tit* and the mellow trilling of the *robin* recall the joys of spring that await us. Come the month of March and the chorus reaches renewed intensity.

But the woods of Essex retain their ornithological interest year round. During winter they belong to *woodpeckers,* colourful *jays* and other hardy residents. Mixed winter flocks of tits rove among the branches, in some areas, most frequently towards the north and west of the county, perhaps including marsh or the increasingly rare *willow tits*. These flocks may conceal other interlopers, seeking to benefit from this safety in numbers. As the birds pass, twittering overhead, a *treecreeper* might catch the eye as it darts down to the base of a trunk, to begin its diligent spiral upwards, all the while searching the fissured bark for grubs. They are decidedly mouse-like, with their inconspicuous brown plumage and squat, scurrying demeanour. That other tree climber, the *nuthatch*, is much more striking: slate-grey back and nape, contrasting the paler, buff tones on the underside. These are agile birds, able to move vertically both up and down, and have an air of elegance that the nonetheless endearing little *treecreeper* lacks.

Similar seasonal gatherings of finches occur. *Redpoll* and *siskin* share a liking for the stands of *alder* associated with damper woodland, while the very observant might be rewarded with the rare glimpse of that most self-effacing and altogether more solitary bird, the *hawfinch*. Even where they occur with regularity, they are notorious for their reluctance to be seen. When sighted they are indeed, unmistakable. As barrel-chested as the *bullfinch*, with a large, conical bill that actually looks strong enough to crush the *beech mast* and other large seeds (and even cherry stones!) on which they feed, this is a bird of singular appearance. The *hawfinch* is an uncommon Essex resident, favouring woods with plenty of *oak, beech* and *hornbeam*. The mature, airy woodland typical of Epping Forest and the old woodland around Danbury provide them with suitable breeding habitat.

The small birds of our woods must be watchful, as hunters are at large. The nocturnal attentions of the *tawny owl* are more relevant for small mammals, but the *sparrowhawk* certainly does pose a very real threat to the woodland avifauna. Their revival following near extinction through the pesticide-instigated declines of the 20th century is thankfully as evident in Essex as elsewhere in the country. Dashing and agile predators, they add a touch of excitement to the woodland scene. They may be seen lurking around woodland clearings, seeking to ambush their prey and maintain the advantage of a surprise attack; the panicked chattering of frightened *blue tits* will often be the precursor to the raptors' appearance. But they are also capable of racing among the trees with seemingly impossible speed and manoeuvrability.

It is the resilience of our resident birds, braving the cold of our winter, which ensures an element of vitality, amid the dormancy and short days of the season until the forthcoming resurgence.

The coming of the spring is celebrated with such sonorous gusto that never fails to delight. The springtime woodland chorus is a thrilling and warming experience. It is a time when the year-round residents redouble their efforts to establish breeding territories and attract mates, when the woods ring with the reassuring sounds of those birds that have stuck out the winter and are present to herald the changing of the seasons.

With the arrival of the summer migrants, returning from their winter sojourn in Africa, the competition for space and sound steps up. Come mid-March, the loud, clear tones of the *chiff chaff* is as eagerly awaited a harbinger of spring as the first *swallow*: barely a wood or copse across the county will see the season through without their cheerful presence. The *blackcap* is similarly widespread. One of our finest songsters, with a penchant for dense scrubby habitat associated with coppiced woodland, their wonderful warbling song, delivered deep in cover from some hidden perch, is so often the first sign of its presence when a sighting may be more difficult to gain.

But few songbirds can be more enigmatic than the *nightingale*, a bird of uncomplicated appearance that is so very much in contrast to the astoundingly melodic and varied song. Like the *blackcap*, the *nightingale* is a bird of thick cover, but although widely distributed in Essex, they are much more thinly scattered. The woodland of the northeast perhaps enjoys the greatest population density. The Stour and Copperas Woods offer opportunity to enjoy an unusual Essex scene, where one can relish the delights of woodland butterflies to the accompaniment of the sweet tones of the *nightingale*, while watching *shelduck* or *oystercatcher* winging their way across a picturesque estuarine landscape. Wherever they occur, their presence can scarcely be missed. Even to the uninitiated, not used to distinguishing individual calls, the song of the *nightingale* will always be recognisable.

Even taking into account the skulking *warblers* and self-effacing *nightingales*, woodland mammals are rarely as evident as the birds. But for the ever-familiar *grey squirrel*, even the more abundant species lead highly secretive lives, invariably under the cover of darkness. Those that brave the light of day tend to do so during the quiet of dusk and dawn and are much too wary to be caught in the open for long.

The mammal life of a wood is therefore a most mysterious component. Not least the *bats* that wing their way impossibly around the night-time woodland. Using sound to see, as high-pitch calls are rebounded back from surrounding objects, providing the bat with a 'picture' of the world, this is a method of perception so complex that such rapid and acrobatic flight can be accommodated in the pitch darkness and even the tiniest insect can be sought out and captured in the blackest of nights. Echo-location really has to be one of the true marvels of nature.

Native woodland is second only to freshwater habitats as an important environment for bats. The *pipistrelle* is the most numerous species in

Essex, as it is nationwide, and even though they are more inclined to roost in old buildings than in trees, colonies may travel some distance to good foraging areas. A tiny species, their fast erratic way of flying over open woodland contrasts with slower more deliberate flight of the *brown long-eared bat*, passing more closely to the vegetation, at times literally plucking their prey from the foliage.

On the ground, rodents like the *wood mouse* and *bank vole* are among the most abundant woodland mammals, but their presence is rarely glimpsed, leaving us instead to guess at the identity of that rustling in the leaf litter in the quiet of the darkening wood: *vole, wood mouse* or perhaps even the lesser known and rather less widespread *yellow-necked mouse.*

Much less likely would it be the *dormouse*, perhaps one of the county's woodland's most important mammal residents. This is a scarce animal of scattered distribution in Essex and currently the focus of much study. A rodent of mixed woodland, with a distinct preference for the denser understorey associated with coppiced woodland, their decline in the last century has been dramatic, largely through the prevalent lack of interest in coppice management at the time. As nocturnal, arboreal creatures they are rarely seen as they deftly clamber among the branches in search of food. And what a varied palate they have. In spring the catkins and flowers of deciduous trees comprise their diet, before taking advantage of the summer abundance of insects. The bonanza of autumn berries and hazel nuts provide the means to fatten themselves up before the winter hibernation.

However, if not the most numerous mammal of Essex woods, it is the *grey squirrel* that is by far the most likely to be seen by the casual visitor. As an American introduction to Britain during the 19th century, they are still often scorned for their role in the extinction of the native *red* over much of its former range. The *red squirrel* survived in Essex until the 1970s – about the same time the *grey* completed its colonisation of the county.

It is nevertheless, difficult not to appreciate what the *grey squirrel* brings to the woodland scene and hard not to admire the resourcefulness of this adaptive little beast. They entertain us with their incredible agility and devil-may-care attitude towards tree climbing, bounding around the treetops as if just the mere possibility of falling to the ground doesn't even enter the equation. They endear us with an undeniably cheeky demeanour and when tame enough to share our picnics they thrill us with the opportunity to quite literally get within touching distance of wild animals. If they were to vanish from our woods tomorrow we would surely miss them.

But while the concealed rustles of rodents frustrate and the mischievous presence of the squirrel adds a touch of cheeriness, it is the larger mammals that perhaps do more to bring a sense of 'wildness' to the woodland scene; to catch sight of them delivers an element of drama. The wolf and bear are long gone, but in the fragments of the ancient wooded habitat that remain there are still beasts that capture some of the grandeur of the wildwood past.

The likes of deer are very wary of human influence on the Essex countryside, but some of our larger mammals tolerate the close presence of humans, and the increasingly urban environment that we bring before us. As well as the *red fox*, an animal so adaptive as to not easily be associated with any one habitat more than another, the *badger* is present throughout the county. Although absent from the very heavily built up areas of metropolitan southwest Essex, they may still be encountered in the encapsulated stretches of woodland in the south.

With such a familiar image, this is a creature that is difficult to confuse with anything else and requires little by way of introduction, but there will be many whose meeting with a *badger*, if realised at all, will consist of a disappearing image of that endearingly ambling gait, shuffling off into the darkness. Signs of their residence in our woods may often prove rather less elusive. A badger sett can be an excavation of considerable extent, incorporating numerous entrances and many tens of metres of tunnels leading to sleeping chambers and latrines – a veritable subterranean maze. They may be used by successive generations, each one adding their own extension, and so can expand almost indefinitely. The record stands at 180 entrances to 880 metres of tunnel and fifty nest chambers.

Those privileged to have observed them at length would surely agree that *badger*-watching is a most rewarding naturalist pastime. Some are fortunate enough to own gardens that encompass a part of their local clan's daily run – *badger*-watching in the comfort of your own home. Others may know of an easily observed woodland sett, where a quiet approach will yield good views. It is the latter scenario that is arguably the more satisfying. In addition to the joy of seeing the animals at close quarters, it is the screeching *tawny owl*, the fleeting glimpse of bats flicking by overhead, or the ethereal blur of nocturnal moths as they drift along the rides that add so much more to the scene and the coolness of the enveloping dusk and the sounds and smells of the darkening wood that make for an all-encompassing experience.

The *badger* is a very 'watchable' creature, with its bustling demeanour and purposeful trot. They are true omnivores, foraging busily for all kinds of plants and animal matter. *Earthworms* are held in particularly high regard, along with such other varied fare as beetles, birds' eggs and fruit. In the later weeks of spring when the cubs are brought above ground they may delight us with their rough and tumble antics, oblivious to the more restrained and wary actions of their watchful parents – a keen sense of smell and incredibly acute hearing more than compensating for poor eyesight. The *badger* is a favourite with so many (except for those who tire of their decidedly un-horticultural approach to garden use) and it is rather difficult to argue otherwise.

It is heartening to know that deer still roam the county. South Essex has become far too crowded for wild deer to tolerate, but in the north and west, where the passing of people is less frequent and where larger tracts of wooded land and relatively less disturbed countryside persist, we may still be privileged with sightings of such beasts.

It is a surprise to many that four species of deer occur within Essex and also that the two we are most likely to encounter are introduced species in Britain, even more so that the most widespread of these is the *muntjac*, a small deer native to China and the only one that has dared to spread into urban reaches of the south.

The second of this pair is the *fallow deer* and, unlike the little *muntjac*, is one that is more likely to satisfy most people's expectations of what wild deer ought to look like. The *fallow deer* is a most attractive animal, in summer clothed in an dappled coat of rich, chestnut-brown fur, the mature buck sporting his impressive, spreading antlers. They move with an elegance that befits a creature that can shift about the trees so swiftly, bounding away with ease into the shelter of the deeper woodland if disturbed by our approach. They inhabit much of the significant wood areas of the county, such as the Forests of Writtle, Hatfield and Epping, as well as much of the wooded habitat of northwest Essex. They owe their presence in Britain, in the most part, to the establishment of medieval deer parks, having been made extinct over much of Europe by the last Ice Age. Of the hundred or so such parks in medieval Essex, few lasted past the 1800s and it is from these that our wild *fallow deer* are descended. Native or not, the sight of these deer in our woods is always a thrilling sight and one that might cause a rush of excitement to the onlooker that goes some way to mirroring the startled, adrenalin-fuelled response that we instigate in the beasts themselves.

Our other two species are the only native British deer, the *roe* and *red*. Both are scarce animals to our county and are perhaps unsurprisingly associated with the relative peace and solitude of the north. The Essex population of *red deer* is particularly small, centred on the Great and Little

Bendysh Woods of the Walden Forest – places that offer the unlikely possibility of viewing four species of deer in Essex. These ancient woods have in the past succumbed to the planting of alien conifers, which the Forestry Commission is now removing in favour of the native broadleaf species. Even if the deer elude, their numerous tracks in the mud betray their presence; the sizeable prints of the *red* conspicuously larger than the lighter set *fallow* and altogether more petite signs of *roe deer* and *muntjac*. The ascending springtime song of the *willow warbler* and its equally vociferous cohorts will also provide further, ample consolation, as will the *oxlip*s and *anemones* dotted along the ride edges.

If the *fallow deer* conveys an air of grace and elegance, then the *red deer* can only be described as the most majestic of all our mammals. A meeting with one is never forgotten. Measuring 1.2 metres at the shoulder and up to two metres in length, they cut an impressive figure. A stag might weigh 250kg, more than twice that of the *fallow deer*, and his antlers may measure seventy or even ninety centimetres across, further generating an image of strength and nobility. The presence of *red deer* in Essex is one the rarest of all our animals. Even though ours are most unlikely to be of true British stock, which are largely now confined to Northwest England and Scotland, the sight of these magnificent creatures in our woodland is no less an embodiment of a wild woodland landscape, the essence of which is preserved in its still surviving descendants.

WOODLANDS IN ESSEX

1. BENDYSH WOODS
(Explorer Map 195/210, Grid Reference 619 398)
A total of 90ha of Forestry Commission woodland, where previously planted conifers are now being removed. *Red, roe, fallow* and *muntjac deer* all use these woods. Birds are plentiful – spring migrants such as *willow warbler, chiff chaff* and *blackcap* can be numerous and *buzzards* may also be seen. The *oxlip* is one of the various ancient woodland plants.

2. BLAKES WOOD
(Exp 183, GR 775 064)
A 42ha National Trust woodland, managed by the Essex Wildlife Trust. This is the site of one of the most spectacular shows of *bluebells* in the county; the earlier display of *wood anemone* is no less impressive. The wood is rich in other flora, with such species as *early purple orchid, great hairy woodrush, moschatel* and *wood spurge*.

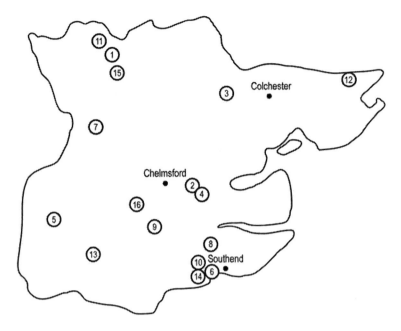

3. CHALKNEY WOOD

(Exp 195, GR 872 273)

Although a large section of this 80ha wood has been planted up with conifers, a part of it comprises the greatest concentration of *small-leaved lime* in Essex.

4. DANBURY RIDGE

(Exp 183, GR 775 064)

A 100ha block of woodland, encompassing areas of heathland and farmland. This is an area of rich and varied flora, home to such plants as *lily-of-the-valley*, *sanicle* and several species of orchid, as well as a number of unusual ferns and sedges.

5. EPPING FOREST

(Exp 174, GR 412 981)

A fine sweep of 2,500ha of woodland, punctuated with open grassy areas and dotted with ponds and riddled with streams. Old *beech* and *oak* pollards survive – the wet areas that adjoin the ponds and streams below contain interesting wetland communities. An excellent site for dragonflies and damselflies – the uncommon *downy emerald* something of a speciality. This is an important area for breeding birds that are scarce elsewhere in the county. *Hawfinch* and *tree pipit* both nest and the *redstart* finds its Essex stronghold here.

6. HADLEIGH GREAT WOOD
   (Exp 175, GR 820 875)

A 37ha nature reserve, home to a thriving population of the *heath fritillary* butterfly.

7. HATFIELD FOREST
   (Exp 183/195, GR 547 202)

A 420ha stretch of historic woodland landscape, offering an insight into what a working mediaeval forest was actually like. Ancient pollards of *oak, beech* and *hornbeam*, plus unusual examples of *maple* and *hawthorn* can be seen. The Forest harbours a fascinating plant life. *Oxlip* and *herb-paris* grow in the coppice and dense clumps of *mistletoe* adorn the trees of the plains. *Fallow deer* still roam and a variety of woodland birds, including the *marsh tit* are also resident.

8. HOCKLEY WOODS
   (Exp 175, GR 833 924)

A fine 108ha area of ancient woodland in the heavily populated south of the county. Another important site for the *heath fritillary*. An excellent wood for birds, with all three species of *woodpecker*, along with *sparrowhawk, tawny owl, nuthatch* and *treecreeper*. A good fungi wood – *death cap, magpie ink cap* and several species of *russula* are among the many.

9. NORSEY WOOD
   (Exp 175, GR 691 955)

A 66ha wood steeped in history, containing many large coppice stools of *sweet chestnut* and *hornbeam*. A varied flora includes a stunning springtime *bluebell* display, while damp stream gullies provide conditions for *willow* and *alder*, dense with pendulous sedge.

10. POUND WOOD
   (Exp 175, GR 816 888)

A 22ha wood, part of an important green swathe in the heart of suburbia. Well-preserved medieval earthbanks hint towards the age of the wood, as do various ancient woodland plants such as *wild service, midland hawthorn* and three species of *woodrush*. A pond harbours large numbers of *smooth* and *palmate newt*, along with several species of dragonfly and damselfly.

11. SHADWELL WOOD
(Exp 209, GR 573 412)

This 7ha wood on the chalky boulder clay of northwest Essex boasts an interesting flora, including *oxlip, herb-paris* and *early-purple orchid.*

12. STOUR AND COPPERAS WOODS
(Exp 184, GR 192 311 & 199 312)

Old woodlands of *sweet chestnut* and *hornbeam coppice* overlooking the picturesque Stour Estuary. Rich in woodland birds and invertebrates, including *lesser spotted woodpecker, nightingale* and butterflies such as the impressive *white admiral* and the canopy dwelling *purple hairstreak.*

13. THORNDON COUNTRY PARK
(Exp 175, GR 716 608)

Covering some 120ha, the park attracts many visitors. As a former deer park, old pollards can still be seen and the northern section contains some fine standard *hornbeam.* Good for winter bird watching, often harbouring large gatherings of finches including *siskin, redpoll* and *brambling.*

14. WEST WOOD (THUNDERSLEY)
(Exp 175, GR 805 880)

A 32ha wood of *oak, hornbeam* and *sweet chestnut,* plus one of the highest concentrations of *wild service* in the county. Many species of fungi appear on the woodland floor in autumn, including various species of *milk cap, russula* and *bolete.*

15. WEST WOOD (UTTLESFORD)
(Exp 195, GR 624 332)

Another of the herb-rich, boulder clay woods of Northwest Essex, with such interesting species as *oxlip* and *wood barley.*

16. WRITTLE FOREST
(Exp 183, GR 638 012)

More than 200ha of privately owned woodland comprise what remains of the forest. Many footpaths lead through atmospheric woodland of *chestnut, oak* and *hornbeam* and areas of secondary *birch* wood. *Muntjac* and *fallow deer* can both be seen, as well as *brown hare* and *little owl* in bordering farmland.

CHAPTER THREE

The Essex Coast and Estuaries: The Last Wilderness

THE EBB AND FLOW

In a part of England as heavily populated and developed as Essex it might seem strange to suggest that we still possess a wild frontier. A true wilderness is usually regarded as a virgin land, pristine and untouched by the comings and goings of human kind; a place where people are merely a transient presence, passing through without any lasting influence. Such areas are obviously hard to find in Britain, 'wilderness' usually only a description reserved for the most remote and desolate of places.

But can it really be described as a wilderness? To the purist, it may perhaps be a difficult case to argue. After all, the coastline itself is a linear place, where the evidence of human activities can often be seen right up to the last few metres of useable land. But by directing your focus towards the empty estuarine landscape spreading out before you, the impression can indeed be one of remoteness. The buoys floating out in the deep water channel might be the only visible clue to human passing. The water ebbs and flows along the shore, just as it has for time immemorial, the birds pass to and fro, responding to the ceaseless rhythm of the tide, a relationship between them and their environment that is centuries old.

Almost at odds with this ageless quality is the constantly shifting profile of the coastline. Human influences aside, the coast more than almost any other habitat is subject to changes brought about by the natural environment. The tireless cycle of the sea destroys and creates in equal measure. As each tide has nibbled away at the soft East Anglian cliffs (in Essex now only found at The Naze, Walton) so the eroded material is washed away and deposited elsewhere. With the calmer waters of our more sheltered stretches of the coast, only the smallest of particles remain suspended. In the relatively still water of a high tide, the sediments are allowed to drop and settle, creating flat expanses of mudflat. With the gently sloping Essex coast these may be of considerable magnitude, sometimes forming the huge sweeps, such as that found off Shoeburyness and Foulness Island. In the even more sheltered waters of estuaries and bays, this mud may escape the erosive effects of tidal currents, allowing pioneering plants such as *cord grass* and *glasswort* to set root. As these new plant communities develop, the successive layers of mud are set down with each tide, and as the level of the reclaimed material grows increasingly higher – eventually beyond the level of the normal high tide – so the plant communities alter accordingly. On other more exposed parts of the coast, where wave action is stronger, larger objects are heaved ashore to build up shingle banks, or perhaps deposited as a narrow spit (as at Colne Point) to the exclusion of the finer sediments.

These habitats are special. Not only do they provide particular conditions for very specialised plants and animals, but unlike other habitats they arise and perpetuate without human intervention. It is not the intermittent influence of humankind, but the ancient movement of the tides that shape them. These are genuinely natural places; a truly wild frontier in a much-changed and semi-natural environment.

The twisting and often extravagantly convoluted Essex coastline winds its way for miles, many more than an initial glance at a map would suggest. We have some 460 kilometres of seawall. Quite some length considering that, as the crow flies, the county scarcely measures more than seventy kilometres from top to bottom. Along its path it is marked by river estuaries, each cutting their own distinct profile. The Thames gapes with open jaws, thirsty to swallow up the returning waters of the incoming tide, the Colne emerges surreptitiously from behind the obscuring presence of Mersea Island, while the narrow estuary of the River Crouch jabs inland back towards its source. Away from these sheltered areas we find the straighter edges or gentle curves of the shoreline smoothed off by the sea.

Undoubtedly seen by some as bland and monotonous, the landward side of the shoreline exhibits a varying backdrop to the coastal scene. Needless to say, an agricultural landscape often predominates, but along the way we find bustling seaside towns, windswept grassland and occasionally, ancient woods. But irrespective of location and circumstance a sense of spaciousness persists. Even along the heavily built-up northern shore of the Thames estuary, where it is hard to imagine a more abrupt transition from the urban to natural, the huge sky and reflective water of the sea (or mudflats, of course, depending on the tide) dominates the scene. The vast flocks of wintering birds that use the expanse of mud as feeding grounds during the winter – stretching from Leigh and Canvey Island to Southend and beyond – often seem indifferent to such close and abundant human inhabitation. Even further upstream at the western edge of Canvey and nearby Coryton, where the sprawling oil refineries glower over the broad tributary of Holehaven Creek, birds still come in numbers, diverting your attention from the surreal and incongruous skyline. Moving north along the shoreline, human presence is unsurprisingly rarely as evident. With the Thames Estuary emerging from the heart of the English capital it was always inevitable that its shores would be susceptible to development. But elsewhere, such as at the wonderful estuaries of the Blackwater and the Stour, we find some of the most remote and peaceful countryside our county has to offer.

What the strange bedfellows of industry and conurbation and the apparent wealth of wildlife in their midst does highlight, however, is the ecological significance of these habitats. There must be something worth returning to each year, in spite of these less-than-salubrious surroundings. The coastal areas of Essex are of national and international renown and comprise some of the scarcest and most biologically productive habitats we have. The intertidal mud is loaded with organic matter, delivered by the outflowing estuarine waters or swept in by the incoming tide. Saltmarsh is a declining habitat in Britain, covering nationally little more than forty thousand hectares, of which maybe four per cent is located around the Essex coast. Shingle habitats are scarce both as a British and European habitat.

Wherever we find ourselves along the maritime fringes of our county, the great ecological significance of the Essex coast has rarely gone unnoticed. The flats and marshes of Leigh, Dengie, the Colne and Blackwater Estuaries and Hamford Water are National Nature Reserves, a combined area in excess of four and a half thousand hectares. A further 848 hectares of the Southend Foreshore has been designated as a Local Nature Reserve. The Essex Wildlife Trust and the Royal Society for the Protection of birds look after many hectares of the remaining Blackwater grazing marshes, the latter rescuing five hundred hectares of this habitat from the hands of developers along the upper Thames Estuary at Rainham Marshes. The Wildlife Trust has also secured the future of shingle and shellbank habitats at Colne Point and Bradwell, as well as areas of grazing marsh and pasture along the Crouch Estuary.

The productivity of these habitats occurs unseen and unknown to most of us, most notably among the muddy seashore and estuaries that support enormous numbers of invertebrates, gorging on the rich supply of phytoplanktonic and algal foodplants. Thousands upon thousands of tiny snails and crustaceans feed on or near the surface. *Lugworms* bury themselves just out of sight, ingesting the surrounding substrate and extracting any nutritional material as it passes through the body, leaving the familiar cast on the surface as clues to their presence. *Ragworms* occupy a different niche, often active above the surface, scavenging and predating upon other smaller invertebrates.

It is the innumerable abundance of lower plants and animals that attracts the huge numbers of birds for which the Essex coast is famous. Relatively few stay to breed, but waders and wildfowl return each winter in their thousands to take their fill of this great bounty and assume their position at the top of the food chain. Clouds of *knot* and *dunlin* swarming excitedly along the line of the falling tide and the skeins of *brent geese*, strikingly black against the background of greys and browns, gliding down to rest on the estuary mud, are among the most wonderful wildlife spectacles in Britain and cannot fail to impress any who witness them.

There is no doubt that for those with ornithological leanings this coast is a good place to visit. There are many spots from which to rattle off an impressive array of birds, often throwing up a rarity or two. However, the natural wonder of coastal Essex goes far beyond mere ticks on a list (although this undoubtedly offers some enjoyment in its own right), but lies within the vastness of the landscapes, where each component part can be viewed almost in full, beneath an all-encompassing sky where nothing is concealed or obscured. Indeed, the perfect situation to contemplate the wildness of your surroundings.

Even landward, where there is no disputing the shaping influence of humans, we frequently find the open arable farmland that, although often of limited wildlife and aesthetic value, allows the spaciousness of the coast to extend inland. Where 'prairie farming' does prevail, the borrow dykes and associated stretches of linear grassland – created through the building of the county's extensive sea defences – offer respite for the wildlife and soft edges for the eye.

In places, an ancient landscape has been preserved where the unimproved pastures of the once extensive grazing marshes have been saved from the rampant drainage and reversion to arable farming of more recent decades. Here the land does more than simply yield to the capacious character of the sea, but its essence is captured and reflected by these windswept grasslands. From a distance they may look flat and faceless, but once among them the hidden detail comes to the fore. Crisscrossing dykes bisect the fields. The open water of broad fleets (created when creeks become isolated from the sea behind the seawall), with their tributaries snaking off into the sward, creates a more significant interruption to the invertebrate-rich tussocky grassland. Wildlife finds a wider range of niches here than the less accommodating arable lands.

With such ingredients in place, coastal Essex can be nothing short of awesome. Some would have it at its best under a brooding winter sky, grey clouds bearing down over the yawning landscape below. On one side the weather-beaten marshlands, sprinkled with grazing waterfowl and probing waders, swirling flocks of *lapwing* billowing into the sky. On the other, the saltmarsh, ridden with runnels wriggling away towards the wader-strewn mudflats. Of the sea beyond we are only given tantalising glimpses of this mysterious world – for the fortunate the privileged sight of an inquisitive *common seal*, momentarily breaking the surface to survey the coastline before disappearing on another long dive. But bathed in the light of the winter sun the scene is equally as inspiring. Now the rippling waters of the marshland fleets sparkle crisply amid frost-coated *reeds*, and estuary waves take on an almost viscous appearance as they break along the silvery mud.

Come the spring and summer, and the ruggedness of winter gives way to an ambience of peaceful solitude. The seashore is now empty of the mass of winter birds, *redshank* and *oystercatcher* among the few waders that maintain a year-round presence, sharing the coast with the ever-present gulls. Without the purposeful mass of feeding birds, the haze that shimmers just above the *purslane*-clad maze of the saltmarsh creates a scene of great calm. The grazing marshes are also without the bustle of hungry winter visitors, the hoards of grazing *brent geese* and *wigeon* having flown north.

But in exchange for the excitement of winter we are given the softness and colour of the milder seasons. Saltmarsh flowers enlighten the scene. Over the grasslands we may be more aware of the smaller birds that inhabit them; *skylark* and *meadow pipit* would have spent the winter, *yellow wagtails* reappearing with the return of more hospitable climes. The non-avian fauna comes to the fore. *Skippers* and *brown* butterflies flit among the grass, while dragonflies speed over the dykes and ditches. What does persist though, irrespective of the time of year, is the pervasive impression of openness, overwhelming enough to infiltrate our very consciousness, imparting to us some of its uncomplicated beauty. These may not seem qualities unique to the coast. Can we not, after all, find such places in the rural interior? Indeed we can, but here we have the reassuring sense of randomness that is so often missing from the carefully organised, pristine fields of Essex farmland.

But as wild and self-perpetuating as they are, our coastal habitats must inevitably resist threats to their well-being. Industry and development bring with them the pressures associated with pollution and inappropriate land use. Industrial contaminants can build up through the food chain and biological pollutants, like sewage, can dramatically upset the natural balance of marine ecosystems.

The influence of intensive agriculture has unfortunately long since diminished the wildlife potential of the terrestrial habitats of our coast.

Marshes have been drained and our ruderal floral and fauna increasingly marginalised by high input farming.

We are now seeing a comparatively new problem facing our coastal environment. As the succession from mudflat to saltmarsh continues its endless cycle, the uncontrolled development of saltmarsh, and ultimately dry land, is regulated by natural forces. The west-east tilt of Britain and the consequently sinking southeastern coast, combined with naturally changing sea currents and altering patterns of erosion, ensure a state of constant flux. But as the sea level rises, possibly also exacerbated by global warming, our valuable saltmarsh habitats are becoming edged out as they meet the immovable barrier presented by our imposing sea defences: 'coastal squeeze' is taking effect. And what a dilemma this presents us with. The wildlife-rich grazing marshes owe their existence to the reclamation of the land made possible by the building of the seawalls, but in maintaining them we compromise the survival of our saltmarshes.

Hopefully with changing attitudes to the coastal environment we may perhaps see a more positive future. So-called 'managed retreat' provides an alternative, in certain instances at least, to the expensive upkeep of our tidal defences. The seawall can be deliberately breached, decreasing the likelihood of flooding in other more vulnerable areas, allowing the sea to reclaim the land behind and restoring the opportunity for the natural succession of our valuable shoreline habitats. At the Essex Wildlife Trust's Abbots Hall Farm on the Blackwater Estuary, the ethos is one of showing how farming can be profitable for farmers and wildlife alike. Managed retreat has taken place, which will in time create new saltmarsh. Elsewhere, grazing marsh is to be reinstated on former arable land and room left alongside the crops to allow wildlife to coexist.

So, is the Essex coast our last wilderness? In some ways, yes it is. These are wild areas that require no help from humans to create, regulate and perpetuate themselves. This is a rarity in our nation of semi-natural habitats, where centuries of human influence have much altered the Essex and, indeed, the British countryside. But more to the point, the answer to this question lies in part with how the individual is moved in the presence of such places. For many, the coastal environment promotes feelings of not just space, but also a sense of freedom, of detachment, at least momentarily, from the stresses of modern existence. In this context they are as much a wilderness as could be wished for. But in spite of their apparent resilience, let us not forget that our coastal habitats are still vulnerable and, at times, fragile places.

It is said by many that among the other wild places of our county the coastal regions are among our most prized assets. The huge wildlife value of these habitats certainly does put us on the ecological map, but in qualitative terms – as a part of the Essex wildlife tapestry – such comparisons are difficult, or even unnecessary to make. We can be sure, however, that these ageless and atmospheric landscapes are among the finest we have.

COASTAL WILDLIFE: RESILIENT AND ADAPTABLE

Those organisms that exist in our coastal habitats have chosen a tough place in which to survive. In places they must withstand a battering from sea and wind, in many they have to tolerate the periodic inundation of the rise and fall of the sea. Other challenges must be encountered. Where nutrients are plentiful in the intertidal mud, the fine, densely packed particles create an anaerobic environment where the acquisition of oxygen is more difficult. On well-aerated shingle banks a lack of sustenance presents the opposite problem.

Through the necessity of survival these habitats have developed unique floral and faunal communities, the component species possessing various adaptations in order that they might survive within their inhospitable environments. The continually disturbed and shifting shingle banks and spits lack the high nutrient levels of the mudflats and estuaries, requiring particular hardiness for any would-be colonisers. Plants of saltmarsh and mud must cope with the unlikely problem of lack of water. The principles of osmosis are based on the movement of water from one body to another along a gradient. If the quantity of water molecules in one body is less than another then water is taken in until a state of equal water concentration is achieved. Thus, the high salt concentration of the seawater and mud draws water out of the plants, requiring of them special mechanisms by which to store or extract water from their environment. Some species maintain higher levels of salt in their cells to enable them to intake water from the saline liquid that surrounds them. Others, like the *glassworts* that inhabit the estuarine mud, possess succulent tissue to aid the storage of water in reserve for times of need.

The animals that dwell in the rich mud of estuary and mudflat must similarly adapt to the harsh and changeable conditions that surround them. Above all, these are places of marked changeability. As the tide ebbs and flows and the rivers flow forth, the creatures that live in the estuary are subject to wildly fluctuating levels of salinity, not to mention the low levels of oxygen inherent in the intertidal mud and the threat of dessication during low tides. Few animals can tolerate the extremes and must, at least to some extent, be able to regulate their immediate environment. Some worms, like the *lugworm*, and molluscs, such as the *baltic tellin*, live and feed in burrows made in the mud, creating microclimates that protect them from the fluctuating conditions above. Other molluscs, like the *edible periwinkle*, seal off their waterproof shells to avoid drying out when left high and dry by the tide.

The periodic and varying patterns of the tide affect a profound influence on the life of the seashore. On the lower reaches, organisms enjoy longer periods of submersion, indeed the deep-water channels will provide permanently submerged conditions. The higher up the shore, the potentially longer are the periods of exposure. On the extreme upper shore, where the latter stages of saltmarsh development have taken place, only the highest spring tides will inundate. Thus, different parts of the shore require different adaptation of the organisms that live in them. The overall effect is one of zonation. Few animals can adapt to the widely varying conditions up and down the whole shore and so certain animals will prevail over others at certain levels.

The huge winter influx of winter wildfowl and waders to our coast is, not unjustifiably, what tends to capture the imagination, and little thought is given to the intriguing interplay of life that takes place further down the food chain. If one does consider our coastal regions as a kind of wild frontier, then the level of adaptation required for plants and animals to exist in such testing environments – although sometimes unspectacular – certainly befits and encapsulates such a perception.

THE SEAWARD SIDE

There can be little doubt that of all the organisms that reside on the muddy fringes of our county it is the birds that attract the most attention. But, as the top consumers, those that smother our shores, year after year, represent the culmination of vastly high levels of productivity that takes place amid the rich, nutrient-loaded mud.

Visit any terrestrial habitat and it is the floral component that initially confronts us. In the wood we must explore the leafy surrounds in order to seek out the animals within, and in the dense sward of the meadow many creatures will evade the less inquisitive. But gaze out across the shining mudflats at low tide and we scarcely miss the apparent lack of obvious vegetation: the seashore, after all, is just about sun, sea and sand, isn't it? But just as in any other ecosystem, plants form the basis of the foodchain here also.

The flora of these muddy expanses, however, is not dominated by the higher plants but almost exclusively by algae. Nevertheless, one of the very few flowering plants that can exist further down the shore, the *eel-grass*, is of particular significance to the Essex estuarine ecosystem, at least to the thousands of *brent geese* that flock to our shores each winter, to which it is an important foodplant. For the most part though, the most noticeable seashore plants are the seaweeds, themselves larger forms of algae. But many of these require solid fixings on which to attach themselves and therefore the mudflat is a poor seaweed habitat. Where solid objects do occur, a few species, like the familiar *bladder* and *knotted wracks*, can set down their holdfasts. Far more important are those species that are barely visible to the human eye. The coastal mud is covered by a film of microscopic algae and it is this that generates substantial quantities of food for the abundant mud-dwelling invertebrates.

Copious worms, crustaceans and molluscs live in enormous quantity on the mud. What they might lack in diversity of species they compensate for in sheer numbers. It really is quite staggering to contemplate that in excess of two hundred thousand organisms can occupy a single square metre of mud. Not only can they gorge on the nutritious algal flora, but also on the huge quantities of organic material brought down river into the estuaries and swept in on each tide. With this knowledge we might look upon the seemingly random probing and dabbling of waders and wildfowl in a rather different light.

Most of us will witness comparatively little of this abundance of lower animals, with so many of their number inhabiting the mid to lower reaches of the shore. There will, nevertheless, be representatives to be found on the upper shore, giving at least an insight into the richness of life that teams beyond. Of the crustaceans, the tiny sandhopper *Corophium* is one creature that occurs *en masse*, burrowing at the surface of the spreading mudflats, but other larger species scavenge among the decaying seaweeds left stranded by the high tide, springing erratically into the air when disturbed. The woodlouse-like *sea-slaters* forage well away from the reach of the tide, scuttling among stones or the crevices of sea-walls and other coastal structures for organic debris.

In the pools left by the falling tide we might observe a more typically marine element of the crustacean fauna. In these shallow waters *shrimps* may become trapped higher up on the shore. Darting away with lightning-fast reactions at the movement of any would-be threat from above, they can leave the onlooker wondering if they are being deceived by a trick of the light on the rippling water. A slower, stealthier approach might just afford a more prolonged glimpse before they zip off, disappearing with a puff as they burrow into the mud. Rarely more than five centimetres in length, these are hardy, adaptable creatures, powerful claws positioned on the foremost pair of legs enabling them to exploit a wide range of prey. Small fish, worms and other crustaceans, as well as plants and any other organic material they might happen upon are all fair game.

More familiar perhaps, are the seashore molluscs. For some species their empty shells are the only really obvious proof of their presence. Bivalve molluscs like the *sand gaper, cockle,* and *tellin* live most of their lives buried in the mud, filtering out organic particles from the surface via extended tubes, their soft vulnerable bodies protected inside a pair of enclosed shells. These shells can sometimes accumulate high up the shore in great quantity, creating shell banks such as that found at the EWT's Bradwell Cockle Spit nature reserve.

We can, however, find still living molluscs in open view on the more upper reaches of the shore, or at least the shells that conceal a hidden creature inside. Mussels stick out periods of low tide firmly encased in a pair of whale-like dark blue, tear-shaped shells. They attach themselves to solid objects, often in dense clusters and encrusted with barnacles, easy pickings for specialist shell-breakers like the *oystercatcher*. When submerged they open up and filter food particles from the water through frilled siphons.

Another species is particularly obvious at low tide. *Edible periwinkles* adhering to any suitable solid surfaces will also await the return of the tide. The tough little shell is able to withstand a fearsome battering by crashing waves. Covered by the tide once more, they go about their grazing habits, rasping away algae from structures and stones and browsing on organic detritus.

Indeed, there is another 'grazer' that is so very important to this intertidal ecosystem, but rarely seen other than by those who seek them out. The *laver spire shell*, or *Hydrobia*, is one of the super-abundant invertebrates that make these muddy havens tick. A single square metre of mud might hold many thousands of these tiny snails, feasting on the nutrient-rich slime that covers the mud, yet at just a few millimetres in length they will more often than not go unnoticed. Unnoticed except by the *dunlin, knot* and *shelduck*, among others, that take their fill each winter.

It seems strange that, considering the peaceful desolation that can be achieved elsewhere in the county, it is the seafront at Southend that places itself in mind when pondering the opportunities for exploring these aspects of our coastal wildlife.

But along the beach – nothing but a thin ribbon of stony sand edging the vast sweeping mudflats of the Thames Estuary – we can seek out the clues to the richness of life away down the shore. *Periwinkles* cling to the breakwaters, and among the numerous cockleshells *slipper limpets* and *peppery furrow shells* may be discovered. There is even the possibility of finding the intact shell-like skeletons, or tests, of *green sea urchins*. On the mud, pimpled by the casts of burrowing *lugworms*, shallow pools at low tide trap *shrimps* and *sand gobies*, the latter being small fish of shallow waters.

Sure, spend too long by the garish colours and abrasive sounds of the amusement arcades and you might possibly go mad. If on the other hand you are merely passing through to reach the famous pier, then it is well worth the temporary assault on the senses. The noise of the pleasure grounds is soon left behind along the boards of the footway. Halfway to the pier head, a kilometre from land, and the sense of openness has flooded in around you. At low tide the rippled contours of the flat sand stretch out in endless tessellation, a high tide and you feel some sensation of being out at sea. Some parts of the pier structure provide an artificial niche for small numbers of *beadlet anemones*, creatures more akin to rocky shores where rockpools provide the perfect environment for their sedentary lifestyle. Retreating into shapeless red blobs when exposed, they blossom with the returning tide, two hundred retractable tentacles wriggling out into the surrounding water.

Only as we come further up the shore do we find the presence of higher plants in any number. As the tidal currents begin to relent along the sheltered shores and estuaries, some will find enough stability in the viscous mud to set root. Only *eel-grass* can really be described as marine species proper, providing an irresistible draw for thousands of *brent geese* that flock to the Essex coast each winter. They are one of the very few groups of truly marine plants. Male and female flowers are borne separately on the same inflorescence, clad in a protective sheath. During fertilisation the thread-like pollen grains are cast into the water, the tidal currents fulfilling the same purpose of wind for their terrestrial counterparts. When coming into contact with the female flowers they curl themselves around the stigma and pollination takes place.

Aside from the exceptional *eel-grasses*, only at the beginning of the succession from mudflat to saltmarsh do other flowering plants begin to occur. Where the saltmarsh fringes the open mud, the flat landscape gains texture, shape and contour. As the flats give way to marsh, the visual warmth of the green-topped banks provide contrast with the smooth, gleaming mud. Where the saltmarsh is allowed to stretch out towards the mud and the open sea, it makes for a wonderfully liberating panorama. Some of the more extensive areas of saltmarsh are to be found along the northern bank of the Blackwater Estuary. Looking southwest from The Strood causeway that connects Mersea Island to the mainland, and a vista of mud and marsh funnels away between the mainland and the island, interrupted only by the unlikely shrubby dome of Ray Island: to the left bending around the coastline of the island, to the right opening out to the lonely marshlands of Tollesbury and Old Hall. It is a landscape that invites you to relish in its invigorating expansiveness.

Much as estuary life in general is layered according to the extent and limits of the tides, saltmarshes themselves are zoned. The *glassworts* and *cord-grasses* are species of the so-called lower marsh community. They are able to tolerate more frequent inundation than those further up the salt-marsh and are two of the classic colonisers of bare estuarine mud, helping to enhance the stability of the substrate and further accumulation of materials.

The creeping habit of the *cord-grasses* provides the perfect means to conquer this shifting environment. Their roots spread beneath the mud giving firm anchorage and aeroid tissue enhances their ability to take in oxygen, allowing them to overcome the anaerobic conditions. As the marsh develops and slowly distances itself from the normal reach of the tide, more species are able to move in, although some may still have to endure the occasional flooding by the extreme high tides and will certainly fall within the influence of the water-sapping salt spray.

As the marsh rises up above its muddy origins it becomes smothered by *sea purslane*. But for their ubiquity, these plants with their rather inconspicuous spikes of little yellow flowers would make for a somewhat unas suming presence, but in number they do much to clothe the creek banks. Others are less understated. The soft hues of *sea-lavender* may paint summer swathes of pastel purple across the carpet of glaucous green, the bright yellow blooms of *golden samphire* provide explosions of colour along the saltmarsh edge, while the yellow-centred purple flowers of *sea aster* provide further decoration.

It seems ironic that so comparatively few animals feed directly on the flowering plants of such biologically rich ecosystems as mudflat and salt-marsh. There are, for instance, only a handful of moths associated with saltmarsh plants, unlike the many dozens connected with say, meadow grasses, and certain notable species of *bush-cricket* such as the *short-winged conehead*. Even so, a proportion of the organic material that drives the productivity of mud and marsh will be derived from the litter of these plants and in this way incorporated into the fertile melting pot and devoured indirectly.

And the pot is brim full. Many tens of thousands of wildfowl and wader flock each winter to take their fill of this extraordinary bounty. If a single duck takes two thousand or more tiny crustaceans in one day, then how many would fifty thousand *shelduck*, *wigeon* or *teal* consume in the course of the whole winter. Yet all the while the muddy stretches of the Essex coast maintain unwavering levels of very high productivity. We may look on this abundance of birdlife as a kind of celebration of this muddy paradise.

If you were to visit the coast for the first time during the spring and summer months, then the scene would be one of a huge empty expanse, dotted with gulls and perhaps a few opportunistic crows and starlings. Few of the waders that crowd onto the winter mud stay in the county to breed. *Redshank*, the so-called sentinels of the marshes by dint of their loud, piping alarm calls, maintain their vigil throughout, company for the *oystercatcher, ringed plover* and the hugely declined *lapwing*.

There has, however, been one recent and much-welcomed addition to the breeding wader list. In the mid-1990s Two Tree Island was the somewhat unlikely location for the appearance of nesting *avocet*. Here is a bird once associated with the tireless conservation efforts of the RSPB, as they nurtured a tiny East Anglian breeding population, which now has chosen to nest among one of the most populated stretches of the Essex coastline. Thankfully the dog walkers and vandals have been kept at bay and the birds have stayed. They are undeniably beautiful creatures: slender in build and ornate in plumage. Yet on their breeding grounds this air of grace can be swiftly exchanged for one of bold aggression when defending a nest. These are birds that are still scarce but doing okay.

If your second visit to the coast happened to be during mid-winter, then the picture would surely amaze you. You would be confronted with thousands upon thousands of birds, so different from the seemingly vacant summer scene. Newly exposed mud might be crammed full of waders, in a feeding frenzy once more, having patiently sat out the inundation of the high tide. *Dunlins*, the most numerous, bustle around as if by clockwork, totally at contrast, in both stature and gait, to the massive *curlews* stalking the mud and probing for worms with that long, curved bill. *Knot* may gather in considerable number. With a rising tide nudging towards its highest point, huge flocks of these and the diminutive *dunlin* swirl up over the flow, agitated from their high-tide roost on the uppermost elevation of the saltmarsh. The dull grey of their plumage may almost be lost against a bleak winter sky, but banking this way and that, as one twisting sinuous shape, their clean white undersides flash brightly against the gloomy backdrop.

To make subsequent visits along the shoreline, then we may be able to appreciate the subtle qualities that gives each area its own distinctive feel. The mud and saltmarsh plants may vary little, and many of our coastal birds are ubiquitous to the main estuaries and other sheltered stretches of our coast, but we are soon able to associate different things with different places, whether through our own personal experiences or the habitats and distribution of the animals themselves. The Stour, for example, has its *pintail*. The drake must surely be one of our most beautiful birds, exquisite with his finely arranged plumage of black, grey and white. Even the predictably drab brown female portrays an air of elegance, not often associated with the ungainly ducks. And while the *brent geese* will be seen along much of the Essex coast, the massed flocks that gather on the mudflats of the Thames Estuary near Leigh on Sea – often as large as five thousand strong – are the ones that might more likely come to mind. The autumn arrival of the geese brings with them a touch of wildness into the heart of urban Essex, their soft babbling calls adding a calming sound to the droning bustle.

There are, of course, those places that are more distinctive. Away from the protective influence of the estuary, where the force of the sea comes to bear unimpeded on the land, there will be no saltmarsh or fertile mud. As the waves haul up stones and shells to build the shingle and shell banks, the much finer organic particles are swept away, leaving a barren and desolate situation. Lacking is the rich substrate to assist the colonisation of plants and thus little potential for animals to move in. But nature will always find a way.

Shingle is a constantly shifting environment, where in addition to the effects of salt spray there is little water and scant organic material, but where there is enough stability there are plants that can survive. Such species as *sea-kale* perhaps have a robustness befitting their uncompromising surroundings, but the colourful blooms of the *yellow horned-poppy* and the unique beauty of the *sea holly* do much to belie the blandness of the shingle habitats. Sadly, these plants and others have become highly localised species among the Essex flora with much of their former habitat having been developed as seaside holiday parks. It is only at such well-preserved shingle habitats like that which we can find at Hamford Water and the Colne Point nature reserve that such wildlife is able to thrive.

Shingle and shell-bank vegetation is rather sparse in nature. Where plants have colonised, their coverage is inconsistent and patchy. The resident birds, however, seek out such conditions. *Oystercatcher* and *ringed plover* both favour these areas to fashion their shallow scrape of a nest, but perhaps the most important bird of these stony places is the *little tern*. Even though past conservation efforts have rescued these summer migrants from the brink as a nesting species, they still remain one of the country's scarcest breeding seabirds. A good twenty per cent smaller than the much more numerous *common tern*, the *little tern* retains all of the aerial grace of their larger cousins. Even when almost lost against the rolling North Sea waves, their buoyant flight still catches the eye among the whitecaps, interrupted with frequent, incisive dives, keen eyes somehow seeking out the fish beneath the surface.

WHERE LAND MEETS THE SEA

The transition from the maritime to the terrestrial is effortless. At some localities we may find gradation from seashore to dry land, incorporating beach and, unfortunately very rarely in Essex, sand dune, but even where the change is abrupt, where the seawall draws a definite line between the shore and the land beyond, the effect is never jarring to the senses.

Unlike the world seaward of the shoreline, the landward habitats, as exposed and weather-beaten as they may be, provide somewhat less exacting circumstances for life. The most consistent feature of the inland coastal habitats is the seawall that accompanies the shoreline along the great majority of its length. Where the all-too-often sterile spread of arable farmland dominates the scene, these grassy strips and their associated borrow dykes can teem with life. Wild plants can thrive along these uncultivated margins. Some are typical of coastal grassland and the likes of *narrow-leaved bird's-foot trefoil, sea clover* and *knotted hedge-parsley* are localised species that favour the seawall banks.

And among the vegetation, animal life abounds. In places reptiles can be a prominent feature, for instance along some stretches of the River Crouch, where *common lizard* and *adder* enjoy the basking and hunting opportunities of the sun-drenched slopes. Here we also find sanctuary for some of the birds that are being edged out of the prevailing farmland. A *skylark* ascends from the grass, almost, it seems, as you are about to tread on it. This may be a diversionary exercise, diverting your attention from a nearby nest on the ground. If scrubby areas have been allowed to develop at the foot of the seawall or along the borrow dyke, then the decreasingly heard request of the *yellowhammer* for 'a-little-bit-of-bread-and-no-cheese' might still drift out along the coastal breeze.

Where the old grazing marshes have remained unadulterated – but for the browsing mouths of decades of grazing animals – and dykes and ditches full of water plants, then we are presented with a wildlife habitat of considerable value. Like the saltmarshes and mudflats beyond, the winter grazing marsh makes for a similarly impressive spectacle.

There is a sense of irony that at such a wild and lonely expanse as the Blackwater marshes, we share this solitude with the thousands of wintering wildfowl and waders. *Brent geese* and *wigeon* graze the sward in great number. As a high tide edges them off the estuary mud they descend. The geese arriving in waves, a few hundred here, a hundred more there, until quite without you noticing, fifteen hundred or a couple of thousand have come to gather before you. The *wigeon* bank in with rather more urgency, the beat of their wings altogether more rapid, flashing the distinctive broad white stripe on the wing as they speed into land. *Curlew* probe the turf for worms as they do for the marine species, their long-necked, stooped profile almost reminiscent of a distant herd of browsing dinosaur on some great prehistoric plain. *Lapwing* and *golden plover* abide each other's company, easily agitated and put to flight, seemingly without reason.

But perhaps not – a passing *harrier, marsh* or maybe a *hen*, quartering the marsh causes the sky to fill with wings. *Grey herons* survey the dykes, the picture of patience, lacking the purposeful bustle of the waders on the mud, as they maintain a watchful stare for movement beneath the surface, their languid movements converted seamlessly into incisive accuracy as they strike suddenly into the water with that spear-like bill. The *snipe* is a much less obvious ditch-side denizen, these small, cryptically brown waders never straying far from cover as they pick their way along the water's edge. They are most often observed when accidentally flushed, the diagnostically long straight beak an obvious clue to their identity as they launch themselves into the air, perhaps letting out a short croak as they go.

As with the estuary mud, the abundance of winter birds is instigated by the richness of invertebrate life held within the marsh. Wet grasslands harbour a wealth of life. Even where they are prone to flooding, a more limited fauna may nonetheless be highly specialised. Wading birds scour the soil for earthworms and grubs as they would the coastal mud for *lugworms* and crustaceans.

With the winter flocks gone, we are scarcely given as obvious a clue to the richness of the marsh. Few of these masses stay into the spring and summer. Of the wildfowl, the *brent geese*, without exception, return to their summer quarters in the far North, while all but very few of the ducks that enlivened the dykes and fleets stay to breed. Essex maintains a very small breeding population of *teal* and *shoveler*, while the likes of *wigeon* and *pintail* have nested only very rarely in the past. *Redshank, lapwing* and perhaps a few *snipe* (most breeding *snipe* in Essex tend to be associated with inland marshes) are all that will regularly remain of the winter hoards of waders.

While this may be seen as painting a rather dull picture of summer on the grazing marsh, the reality is very different. Resident and migrant passerines ensure the continued ornithological interest. A delicate 'peep-peep-peep' alerts us to the presence of the *meadow pipit*, as they flit between the ground and fence posts. *Reed buntings* zip to and fro among the weather-beaten shrubs and rustling reeds, the black-headed male a handsome little bird with his white collar and moustache. The *reeds* that line the dykes and fleets may become infiltrated by the babbling song of the *reed warbler* as they arrive back for the summer. In places the swaying stems of this most distinctive grass have attained considerable coverage, such as around the Blackwater Estuary and Wat Tyler Country Park, so much so as to attract such scarce reedbed specialists as *Cetti's warbler* and *bearded tit*. Like the *reed warbler, yellow wagtails* also make a return from their Southerly wintering grounds, surprisingly inconspicuous in spite of their vivid coloration as they scurry among the grass, searching the blades for insects, much much as their *pied* cousins might on our playing fields and parks.

Mammals are as frustratingly elusive as anywhere else. The small mammals that attract the watchful *harriers* and *short-eared owls* in the winter stay well out of the human gaze. The *brown hare*, however, that has declined over so much of the countryside, seem to find these grazing lands, and in places the farmland also, most favourable to their needs. Indeed, along stretches of the Crouch Estuary, one almost expects to see that lumbering gait, far too rangy to be a rabbit, as it negotiates the tussocks and furrows.

Insects are scarce in the seaward habitats, entirely so in those that are truly marine in nature, but among the vegetation of the adjacent grazing lands and vegetated sea defences they find ample opportunities to thrive. Of the hidden invertebrate wealth of the species' rich sward, the *small heath* butterfly offers a more visible presence. Although insects with no really distinct leaning towards any particular type of grassland, they are species very much at home on the livestock-nibbled coastal grasslands, providing conditions are not too wet.

Moths inevitably outnumber the butterflies and include certain coastal specialities. The *cream-spot tiger*, although catholic in its choice of food-plant, shows a decided preference for coastal areas. The strikingly marked black and yellow adults are rarely seen through casual observation. The late summer invasion of their 'hairy jack' caterpillars, however, are hard to miss as they perilously traverse the open ground, often relying on the keen eyes of the walker to avoid an untimely end beneath an unknowing boot, such may be their number in favoured spots.

There is another species, though, that is truly an Essex speciality. On the narrow leaves of the *hog's fennel* feeds the caterpillars of *Fisher's estuarine moth*. The golden brown upperwings adorned with several irregular white spots offer as subtle a beauty as one might expect from an insect of the large *Noctuid* family, typified by the cryptic coloration of many of its members. The foodplant itself is one of Britain's rarest plants. The tightly packed, faintly yellow pom-poms that comprise the characteristic umbels can be seen only around the coastal lands of north Essex and north Kent. The moth associated with them occurs only at the former, where insects and plant thrive around the borders of Hamford Water.

Orthoptera inevitably thrive, more so in areas that escape the browsing mouths of livestock. The *meadow grasshopper* is a ubiquitously abundant species, but as with the *Lepidoptera*, there are those that are well known from their coastal haunts. None are exclusively tied to these regions but such species as the *lesser marsh grasshopper* and *Roesel's bush-cricket* occupy much of their range among grassy habitats of the coast.

The dykes are magnets for insects, heaving with the aquatic *tasselweed* and perhaps adorned by the white sprinkling of *water-crowfoot* flowers spreading across the surface. Attracted by the clouds of tiny flies, dragonflies race up and down their linear territories, impervious to the withering summer heat as they chase down their prey. The water may be brackish, rendering them unsuitable to many species.

Some though, are less fussy. *Migrant hawker* and *common darter* ensure that the marshes are not without the excitement that these wonderful creatures bring to the countryside. In the less robust damselflies we find a special creature with a penchant for the well-vegetated pools and ditches of the Essex grazing marshes. The *scarce emerald damselfly* was once feared extinct in Britain, although in truth they may have merely been overlooked, as they no doubt still are today, given their similarity to the much more common and widespread *emerald damselfly*. They are still nevertheless, a rare creature, much less numerous than their more lightly built close relative. When the massed hoards of winter birds depart to spread themselves more thinly around their breeding grounds, these little green gems do much to remind us of the hidden, year-round magic of the Essex coast.

THE COAST AND ESTUARIES OF ESSEX

1. BARTONHALL CREEK / RIVER ROACH
(Explorer 175, Grid Reference 919 913)

Somewhat overshadowed by the attractions of the nearby Thames and Crouch Estuaries, the Roach is nevertheless a pleasant and productive place to visit. Winter visitors include all the usual suspects, like *brent goose, wigeon* and *grey plover*, while such migrants as *whimbrel* and *common sandpiper* might stop over during the autumn passage.

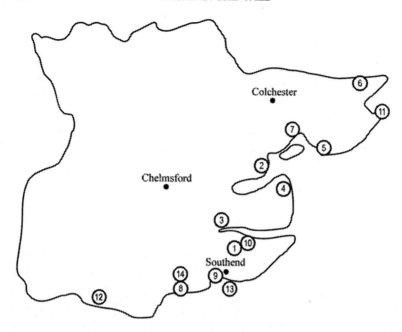

2. BLACKWATER ESTUARY
    (Exp 176, GR 970 104)

Glorious expanse of grazing marsh, saltmarsh and estuary waters. Numbers of wintering wildfowl are impressive, with masses of *wigeon* and *teal*, plus *shoveler* and *pintail*. The sight of hunting *harriers* completes the spectacle. The estuary may yield sea ducks, such as *scoter* and *merganser* and glimpses of *common seal*.

3. BLUE HOUSE FARM
    (Exp 175, GR 856 971)

A 249ha Essex Wildlife Trust working farm on the northern shore of the River Crouch, consisting mainly of grazing marsh with a large fleet. Many *brent geese, wigeon* and various waders including *lapwing* and *golden plover* use the farm at high tide. *Brown hare* are frequently seen. The dykes harbour *water vole* and uncommon *Odonata*, namely *scarce emerald damselfly* and *hairy dragonfly*.

4. BRADWELL / DENGIE PENINSULA
    (Exp, 176, GR 035 081)

Wonderfully lonely part of the Essex coast, a befitting haunt for the *raptors* and *short-eared owls* that visit in the winter months. Extensive saltmarsh and mudflat attracts huge numbers of winter waders and a 12ha shell bank holds breeding *little tern, ringed plover* and *oystercatcher*.

5. COLNE POINT

(Exp 184, GR 108 125)

A splendid 273ha nature reserve of saltmarsh, sand dunes and one of the best shingle spits in Essex. Many waders, wildfowl and raptors are present in the winter. *Little tern* nest and interesting passage migrants might pass through in due season. *Sea holly* and *yellow horned-poppy* comprise part of the interesting shingle and dune flora.

6. COPPERAS BAY

(Exp 184, GR 195 318)

This 287ha RSPB nature reserve encompasses a section of the picturesque Stour Estuary below a wooded stretch of the south shore. Of the numerous waders and wildfowl that use the bay in winter, *black-tailed godwit* and *pintail* are notable.

7. FINGRINGHOE WICK

(Exp 184, GR 041 195)

Former headquarters of the Essex Wildlife Trust, abutting the shore of the Colne Estuary. These former gravel workings are now recolonised by woodland, heath scrub and reed, also containing several lakes and ponds. Huge variety of wildlife to be found. Butterflies include *green hairstreak*, a number of species of dragonfly and damselfly breed in the many pools, while *stoats* hunt the numerous rabbits. Birdlife abounds and this is one of the best places in the county to see *nightingale*. Hides overlooking the estuary give fine views of the extensive Geedon Saltings. At high tide, *grebes* and *merganser* frequent the estuary and large numbers of waders and wildfowl roost on the saltmarsh.

8. FOBBING MARSH

(Exp 175, GR 732 846)

An important area of Thameside grazing marsh and rough grassland. The marsh is well used by winter birds and numerous dykes provide habitat for the scarce emerald damselfly.

9. LEIGH AND BENFLEET

Viewed from Two Tree Island (Exp 175, GR 824 852) extensive mudflats attract huge numbers of waders and wildfowl, including many thousands each of *dunlin* and *knot* and important numbers of *brent geese*. The rough grassland of the island itself rings with the song of *skylark* in spring, when the scratchy warbles of *whitethroat* and *sedge warbler* are also heard. A small area of grazing marsh lies within Hadleigh Castle Country Park

(Exp, 175, GR 799 870). *Snipe, teal* and *shelduck* are present during winter, when flocks of *curlew* stalk the grassland at times of high tide. The dykes and ditches are home to *scarce emerald damselfly* and a substantial population of the introduced *marsh frog. Little grebe* and *coot* breed in the borrow dyke.

10. LION CREEK AND LOWER RAYPITS
    (Exp 175, GR 923 948)

Two EWT reserves provide an opportunity to enjoy a most peaceful stretch of the River Crouch. The scrub around Lion Creek may harbour breeding birds, such as *whitethroat*, and passage migrants like *whinchat* may stop by in late summer. *Adders* and *common lizard* inhabit the rough grassland. *Barn* and *short-eared owl* have been seen quartering the pasture at Raypits.

11. THE NAZE, WALTON
    (Exp 184, GR 264 235)

The scrubby, rabbit nibbled grassland of The Naze, as well as being a prime site for passage migrants, also allows uninterrupted views over the marvellous Hamford Water, with its spreading saltmarsh and the open North Sea. Hamford Water holds the most important *little tern* colony in the county and also the rare umbellifer *hog's fennel,* itself devoured by the even rarer *Fisher's estuarine moth.* Scouring the open sea may bring sightings of passing seabirds, such as *common scoter.*

12. RAINHAM MARSHES
    (Exp 162, GR 535 800)

An important area of the inner Thames Marshes in the shape of a five-hundred hectare swathe of this RSPB reserve. Winter numbers of waders and wildfowl are a prominent feature but the grazing marsh and ditches are home to a range of wildlife, including many wetland plants and invertebrates and a large population of *water vole.*

13. SOUTHEND PIER
    (Exp 175, GR 885 850)

This two-kilometre-long pier provides a vantage point for some excellent seabird watching as it juts out across the 848ha Southend Foreshore Local Nature Reserve. *Terns* and *skuas* pass by on autumn passage, while *auks* and *divers* occur in winter. Among the numerous cockle and mussel shells, *slipper limpets* and *peppery furrow shell* can be found.

14. WAT TYLER COUNTRY PARK
   (Exp 175, GR 739 867)

A 50ha country park bordering Vange Creek, connected to the Thames Estuary via Holehaven Creek. A large fleet, scrape and extensive reedbed border thorn woodland and grassland. *Water vole* and *water rail* lurk among the reeds where a number of *reed warblers* nest. Interesting waders can turn up on the scrape during passage times, including *ruff, green sandpiper* and *spotted redshank.*

An ebbing tide at Benfleet Creek

The *comma*, so called for the comma-like mark on the underside,
is also easily recognised by the jagged edges to its orange-brown wings

The *common ground hopper* is a small and inconspicuous relative to the grasshopper, often found on heathland

Chigborough Lakes: a fine gravel-pit nature reserve

The ornately beautiful *herb-paris*

The bright yellow blooms of *golden samphire* light up the summer saltmarsh

The orange and brown wings of the *gatekeeper* are a late summer delight

Black spleenwort is one of
several species of fern to be
found at Stow Maries Halt

Yellow iris provide striking colour
to river bank and pond edge

Sunbeams slice through the shade of the tree canopy at Hockley Woods

Dunlin gather in great number to feed on the rich mud of the Essex coast and estuaries

Bramble blossom is irresistible to the *white-letter hairstreak*

Whether with petals that are pink or almost white, the *common spotted orchid* always sports a beautiful flower spike

A *ruddy darter* takes a moment to bask in the heat

Oxlips are an indicator of ancient boulder-clay woodland

Roesel's bush-cricket is often present on the coastal grasslands of Essex

Meadow buttercup and *early-purple orchid* create a blaze of colour at Oxley Meadow

The pink flowers of the *red campion* can often be seen dotted along the roadsides and hedgerows

Early-purple orchids might be seen growing in impressive stands beneath the tree canopy

Interlopers from the Continent, *marsh frogs* are quite at home at Hadleigh Marsh

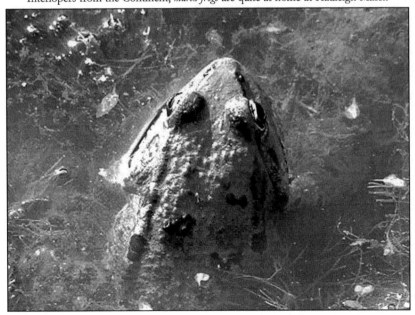

Green hairstreaks are a springtime feature of the heathland at Danbury Common

Common twayblade is one the less
conspicuous of Essex orchids

Wildlife and industry: birds still flock to the mud of Holehaven Creek,
despite the sprawling oil refinery

Adder's-tongue fern is an oddity
of Essex grasslands

The shimmering blue of the *banded demoiselle* is a familiar sight along many Essex rivers

The rare and exquisite *heath fritillary*

Edible periwinkles exposed at high tide

The impressive *emperor moth*

The *field grasshopper* is one of the most common and widespread in the county

The *purple hairstreak* only occasionally descends from the treetops
to show off the purple sheen of its upperwings

A *redshank* delivers its far-carrying call

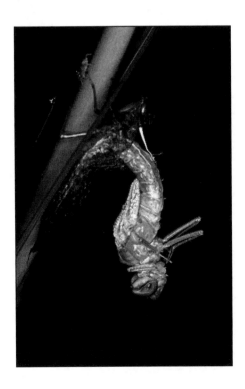

An adult *emperor dragonfly* emerges
from its larval skin

The *death cap* is is ominous as it sounds: deadly, with no known antidote

Common seals hauled up in the Thames estuary

Bluebell plus *peacock* – a picture of spring

A *common lizard* soaks up the sunshine

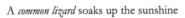

A *common toad* on the prowl

The introduced *muntjac* has now colonised much of the county

Iridescent green and tipped with pastel blue, the scarce *emerald damselfly*
is a jewel of Essex grazing marshes

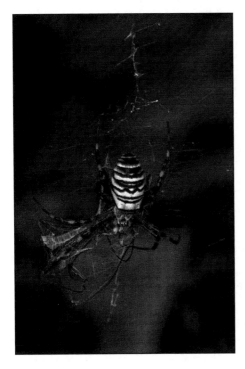

The female resplendent with yellow,
black and white striped abdomen, the
wasp spider is a stunning creature

Waxwings can bring a touch of the exotic to the urban landscape

The tall spikes of the *foxglove* relish
the sunshine of the open coppice

CHAPTER FOUR

Wildflower Grasslands and Heather Heaths: Jewels of the Essex Countryside

HUMAN CREATION BY NATURE'S DESIGN

Flower-rich grassland and lowland heath – definitions perhaps with a certain degree of ambiguity. For the purposes of this chapter, the wildflower grasslands referred to are those areas of old meadow or pasture that have survived the centuries of change, often through the continuation of age-old management regimes, with their rich assemblages of grasses and herbaceous plants intact. Often it is that such ecosystems exist entwined and in unison with areas of rambling scrub or the linear habitats of the hedgerow. It may perhaps seem odd that they should be treated here, but so often do their number add to the grassland scene that they can easily be considered typical features – the trickle of birdsong filtering out over meadow vegetation or the *gatekeeper* butterflies reluctant to stray from the shrubby fringe. Similarly the exploration of the heather-dominated lowland heaths must also encompass, in part, the presence of their own distinctive grassland components and the secondary woodland with which they have come to share the countryside.

Although treated together, these habitats will present us with very different situations. The former conjures an image of gently rustling grasses and meadows sprinkled with the varied colours of wildflowers – the latter dominated by swathes of heather and the bright yellow of *gorse* in full bloom. With one, we may associate the dance of summer butterflies, with the other, perhaps, skulking reptiles and equally self-effacing, scrub-loving birds.

Yet despite their clearly different qualities, both owe their respective places in our countryside to a common origin. Were it not for the past and indeed present activities of humans we would not have them at all. Some of Britain's grassland and heath may have occurred naturally, such as in certain coastal areas where the effects of salt spray, paucity of water and buffeting by the wind would have prevented the natural succession to woodland.

In Essex, as was the case over much of the country, such open vegetation could only become established and continue to persist as a product of woodland clearance and the subsequent grazing of animals and other agricultural practices.

So it is with some irony that from the open heathland we gain a sense of timelessness to match that of our ancient woodlands. We might imagine these places existing amidst the wildwood, cutting swathes among the forest lands, lush green with stands of bracken, ablaze with sweeps of flowering heather, trodden by roaming beasts long before the spread of human kind across the land. The reality is that, as ancient as they are, the creation of the lowland heath over much of the southern half of England dates back a mere three and a half thousand years, thanks to the efforts of early Neolithic and Bronze Age farmers (although less dramatic clearances may have occurred during earlier Mesolithic times).

Thus we are reminded that lowland heath is one of the most semi-natural of all our 'semi-natural' habitats, but over the centuries it has nevertheless developed distinctive and valuable wildlife communities with their own uniqueness. Heaths are atmospheric places. In Essex some of their minuscule acreage has survived as common land, where grazing by commoners ensured that the open conditions persisted. They will typically be irregular in outline, as clearly highlighted by the unpredictable perimeter of Galleywood Common near Chelmsford, seemingly fitting in, however it can, among the surrounding plots.

In actuality, this is very much the case, occupying as they do the land left over once the extent of the neighbouring private properties had been delineated. It is this that helps to give these heathy enclaves their rambling quality, one that encourages the exploration of their hidden recesses. These commons tend to be well used by local people in the present day, not for livestock but for recreation, yet the jumbled mosaic of open heath and recolonising woodland allows them to retain a level of intimacy, in spite of the visitor pressures they invariably face.

The vegetation that thrives on the heath typifies the infertile substrate below. *Heathers, gorse* and *birch* all possess mechanisms for extracting scarce and vital nutrients from soil, allowing them to thrive where others fail. With infertility there is acidity. The base nutrients are leached away through free-draining sandy soils, the lack of a rich woodland flora restricting the replacement of organic matter back into the ground.

These are circumstances, though, that are still subject to the natural vegetative succession back to the climax woodland, something that has contributed to the dramatic retraction in area over the last two centuries. Between 1800 and 1983, seventy-five per cent of British heathland was lost. Conversion to agriculture and urban development accounted for the great majority of this loss and although some areas remained undeveloped, the way they were used changed. With the appearance of modern alternatives, commoners relied less and less on the heathland peat and timber for fuel and stopped using *heather* to thatch their roofs and *bracken* for livestock bedding. They inevitably reverted back to woodland, which itself was increasingly regarded as a more viable prospect than the open heath. Not a bad thing, as some might say. After all, deciduous woodland is a valuable and productive habitat in itself. But over the centuries of their existence the lowland heath had come to occupy an important place in the ecology of the British Isles. Thus the remnants that survive today require ongoing management to ensure their survival alongside our majestic woodlands.

In Essex, heathland is a scarce habitat. Only in small fragments can we marvel at the wondrous summertime display of the pink blooms of flowering cushions of *heather*, or the yellow *gorse* blossom, suffusing the air with the rich scent of coconut and whose thorny branches might burble with the rich warbling of *blackcap* and *garden warbler* and perhaps even *nightingale*, who find shelter among the spines. At Danbury Common we find one of the most extensive patchworks of heath, grassland and woodland, and in Tiptree there is one of the finest remaining heathland areas left in Essex. At such places we can witness at first hand the wealth and variety of these environments and enjoy the open space among the comfortable wooded surrounds. These are havens well known by the general public but also where it is easy to find some out-of-the-way corner for private appreciation. From our heathlands we can derive a quality of experience that belies their restricted presence in the Essex landscape.

Sadly, the demise of our flower-rich grasslands provides us with a similarly gloomy history of demise and abuse. A startling decline in excess of ninety per cent has befallen the permanent grasslands across county and country throughout the last two centuries, a great deal of this since the Second World War. Much was lost under the plough in the name of agricultural intensification, most of what survived either being 'agriculturally improved' through the application of organic fertilisers and herbicides, or re-seeded to bring higher yields. Needless to say, both operations leave little or no space for the rich variety that would otherwise prevail.

As with the heathlands, only in exceptional circumstances would a grassland flora represent the climax vegetation, when the conditions curtail the establishment of woody plants, perhaps where soils are naturally infertile, dry, or in very exposed situations.

Indeed, the more diverse assemblages of species are found to occur on the less fertile soils. Following the early woodland clearances the species that would have lived a marginal existence amid the wildwood would have been able to spread throughout the countryside as the world opened up before them, in time generating rich floral and faunal communities of their own.

Grassland communities can develop on a variety of soil types, unlike the sandy, nutrient poor soils associated with lowland heath. Nevertheless, the surface geology that underlies the vegetation of Essex, bears a considerable influence over the species composition of the county's flora, a fact particularly well illustrated by the distribution of grassland plants. A glance at the geological map of Essex shows a clear northwest/southeast divide in soil type. As the glaciers extended south during the last Ice Age their progress was halted by an area of high ground known as the Danbury-Tiptree Ridge. The scouring effect of the advancing ice gouged out the calcareous material as it came, dumping it further south, leaving what we now call Chalky Boulder Clay. Beyond the ridge the London Clay dominated geology of the south and alluvial deposits of the Thames Basin remained, but for the outwashing of some material as the ice melted. The result on the county's flora is significant with a number of species, such as, for example, certain orchids, exhibiting a strong northwesterly bias to their distribution.

Like the heath, if not for the human interference on the unrelenting forces of vegetative succession, grassland would be lost to encroaching scrub and the inevitable woodland coverage. The ecological richness of herb rich grassland lies within its management. For centuries, many grasslands would have been managed in such a way as to allow the coexistence of wildlife with the practical needs of the farmer. The sward might have been left to grow, unfettered from the latter weeks of autumn through until late spring or early summer. The meadow flowers could proliferate, adorning every square yard with colour; mixed purples, pinks, yellows and white – garish combinations in the wrong hands, but always perfectly applied by nature's palette. Come the hay cut and the flowers have set seed. Subsequent grazing of the sward ensures an open and diverse plant community for the following year. Such was the importance of good hay crop to sustain livestock throughout the winter that the hay meadow would have warranted their presence on the best land available to the farmer and may have been used again and again over considerable periods. The best wildflower grasslands that have survived into the present day are those ancient meadows that have never been ploughed and where the traditional methods of management have perpetuated over the long years.

In spite of their dramatic disappearance from the countryside, fragments remain across our county – less limited than our heathlands that are more or less restricted to the southern half of the county. Like their woodland counterparts, the increasing isolation of the surviving species rich grasslands creates a distinction between them and the stark landscape beyond that is much more clearly defined.

In the pockets of rural Essex where wildflowers retain a tenuous presence, their vibrancy is something to treasure. Perhaps a small corner bounded by luxuriant, old hedgerows – stockades to the plight beyond. Alas, this is the state in which we find a great many of Essex's surviving flower-rich grasslands, but in them we can find a riotous celebration of colour. A timely trip to Oxley Meadow, for instance, would surely stop any visitors in their tracks in order to admire the scene before them. We are greeted by a two-and-a-half hectare spread of *meadow buttercup*, infiltrated and perfectly complemented by the rich purple of *green-winged orchids* creating their amethyst drifts throughout the meadow. A breath of wind causes the sward to gently ripple, each multitudinous yellow flower nodding its agreement, in recognition of its contribution to the stunning display that they set out before us.

In places there may even be rare swathes of many hectares. On the sun-soaked slopes of the Benfleet Downs, with their commanding views of the River Thames, the sward grows thick on the fertile clay, littered with *vetches* and *agrimony*, swaying in the summer breeze with the fluidity of an ebbing tide. Across this imaginary sea, the assorted *brown, skipper* and *blue* butterflies skip over the feathery surf of flowering grasses, along shorelines of thorny scrub full of the churring warblings of *whitethroats*.

While not offering up the same sense drama of the coast, or the intimacy of the woodland, there are few places that capture the spirit of an English summer more than a field full of wildflowers. Relishing the rays of the July sun, the heat of high season is perfectly reflected by the intense buzz of life among the grass blades. The wildflower meadow occupies a place in most of our imaginations as a quintessential component of the British countryside, yet the contradiction persists that ancient and unimproved grasslands are such very scarce habitats in our countryside, certainly in Essex. The rich, flower-strewn grasslands and their heathland counterparts are indeed jewels that gleam from within their all-too-frequently developed surroundings. We must be grateful that their delightful presence has not been lost entirely.

THE WILDLIFE OF GRASSLAND AND HEATH: THE EMBODIMENT OF A SEASON

There can be no denying that these are places synonymous with the reassuring warmth of spring and the heat of summer. Their winter dormancy is almost tangible. For the naturalist, of course, it matters not. The teeming Essex coast provides us with a winter draw, and while our estuaries experience their time of heightened activity, the heath and meadow are steeling themselves for their own flurry of rampant growth and resurgence.

Save for the likes of crows, winter thrushes and probing *green wood-peckers* foraging among the turf, the wildflower meadow is an empty, almost barren place during the short days and long nights. The heaths are equally as quiet, but for the roving flocks of tits and finches that might pass through the secondary woodland. But as soon as the rays of the sun attain a level of warmth enough to trigger the first signs of the vernal season we are left with the feeling of a spring ever so slowly beginning to uncoil. Even when the wintry conditions return for a final blast there remains a sense that nature is just biding its time through a temporary inconvenience.

On the open heath, with the sounds of the first of the year's *chiff chaff* ringing out among the *birch* trees, movement among the *heather* begins, once more, to catch the eye. Spiders scurry across the open ground and bumblebees zip among the permanently flowering *gorse* bushes in search of an early nectar supply. *Adders* make their first tentative steps (figuratively speaking) out of hibernation into the spring sunshine, but never far from cover. Out on the meadows the *blackthorn* yields a blaze of white blossom in the bordering hedgerow and scrub. *Cowslip* and *cuckoo flower* provide a sprinkling of colour among the awakening sward, tended by the inquisitive fluttering of *small white* and *orange tip* butterflies. So begins the escalating trickle of emergence towards the later explosion of life and colour.

A Floral Treasure Chest

There are few better ways to while away a few hours in the glorious sunshine than to amble through some lush meadow, with your eyes sifting through the sward, picking out the numerous species of wildflowers and grasses as you go. It is one of the true delights of the countryside and in the islands of diversity around the county we can search out and discover the wonderful variety on offer. We can enjoy the pleasures of damp riverside pastures, home to *meadowsweet* and *cuckoo flower*, or dryer meadows, complete with *yellow rattle*, cut for hay. There are grasslands at their best in spring where the spread of *meadow buttercup* can astound, or those reaching their peak in the heat of early summer, their pleasures augmented by the clouds of butterflies that live and feed among the meadow grasses and flowers. There will of course be the more ubiquitous species of plant that ensure a familiar presence across the county, but in journeying through the pockets of grassland dotted around the four corners of Essex, we might come to appreciate the subtle distinctions among our floral treasures.

To the south there are the slopes of the Hadleigh and Benfleet Downs, rising conspicuously above a landscape dominated by the yawning Thames Estuary and the flat lands of its floodplain. Although partially given over to woodland and scrub, here we find some fine cattle-grazed grassland, adding a great deal to the extensive views that can be had across the town and country below.

As we descend through the woodland that crests the slopes and down onto the late spring sun-drenched grassland, we are given to appreciate a large part of what makes these habitats so special. Leaving the cool closeness of the trees, the heat of the day floods in around you, the hum of life which it sustains filling the open space. Out of the wood you take in a *bramble*-dotted field (conditions intended to favour the rare *shrill carder bee*) hedgerow and scrub and sweeps of open grassland.

And among the *crested dog's-tail* and *Yorkshire fog*, vetches sprinkle their assorted yellow and pink colours among the sward. The yellows are provided by the loose bunches of *meadow vetchling* flowers, a species that is one of our more common vetches, but others are more unusual, like the *grass vetchling* whose grass-like leaves are lost among the blades proper, leaving the vivid pink of their flowers seeming to float randomly among the vegetation.

Lesser knapweed grows throughout, a big favourite of the abundant butterflies and *burnet moths* that gorge on its nectar. The yellow flowered spikes of *agrimony* are a similarly frequent occurrence. So too are the purple decorated heads of the *self-heal* and the rather less obvious pink of *red bartsia*. Of the many grasses found here, such species as *meadow foxtail, creeping bent, cock's-foot* and *rough meadow grass* are all common and widespread throughout the county. Here is a place where we are provided with an impression of the grassland flora over much of this part of the county. A place where we can appreciate the copiousness and colour that our thankfully common species can bring, but also where less common plants can thrive and where rare plants can still be found.

There are, however, absentees from what is obviously a rich flora. Even though the more northerly grasslands of Essex will be more likely to hold wild orchids, such species as *common spotted* and *green-winged* do occur in the south. We would be forgiven for expecting to find them among this varied grassland. This, though, brings to the fore something of the great fascination of the natural world. Through its unpredictability and quirkiness we can never be quite sure of what we will find; this is a world of pleasant surprises.

Orchids are, it can be said, something of an enigma in themselves and we need only travel a stone's throw from splendour of the Hadleigh Downs to the nearby Shipwrights Wood before we encounter them. This is unsurprisingly a predominantly woodland site and a fine one at that; sheets of *bluebells* cover the ground in spring, one of a number of ancient woodland plants that grow here. It is nevertheless a small area of mead-owland abutting the wood that sets Shipwrights apart from a number of other woods in the area. The *common spotted orchid* is our most numerous and widespread species. Those that grow here are few in number, but a host of other plants fill the meadow. The white umbels of *wild carrot* hover above the shorter meadow plants and *ox-eye daisies* abound with their cheery, summertime faces. More unusual are the *musk mallow* and *hairy St John's-wort*.

The *green-winged orchid* takes us further west, to the southern edge of the sprawl of Basildon new town. Within the boundaries of the Langdon Hills Country Park small areas of species-rich grassland have survived and barely a kilometre south of the Country Park lies a remarkable little nature reserve. The single hectare of Horndon Meadow, slotted into a corner created by the bend in the adjacent road, is crammed with wild-flowers. This tiny hay meadow may never even have been ploughed, let alone agriculturally improved. Bordering hedgerows shut away most of the outside world and within their bounds thrives a colony, hundreds strong, of the increasingly scarce *green-winged orchid*, sharing the spring sward with *yellow rattle* and the curious little a*dder's-tongue fern*.

In many ways it is little Horndon Meadow that epitomises the place of the wildflower-scattered meadow and pasture in the modern Essex countryside. Here we find urban and agricultural development all within close proximity, but in the confines of this remnant of another age of land management there persists a quite marvellous array of colour and variety. It reminds us of what is possible if we were only to give nature enough space to weave its wonderful tapestry.

On the boulder clay further north, other species of orchid adorn the grasslands. Troops of *pyramidal orchids* can still be seen at favoured spots, such as at the Sweetings Meadow nature reserve, but their neatly conical, pink flower heads are all the same, a rare sight in Essex. The *bee orchid* rather less so, but they are still nonetheless, uncommon and sporadic in distribution. We will find few less beautiful and engaging flowers in the Essex countryside. With each single flower designed to attract bees by which to be pollinated, three pink petals frame the mimicking part of the bloom: a velvet brown, delicately marked swollen lip. The irony is that British *bee orchids* are rarely pollinated by the insects they have gone to great lengths to attract, almost always being self-pollinated. How different is the *twayblade*. Self-effacing spikes of green flowers require much closer attention if we are to appreciate their more understated delights.

Among this more calcareous sward we will still find the plants of the wider Essex countryside, the *ribwort plantains* and the *common sorrels*, but aside from the orchids, other plants contribute to this subtly different ambience. The delicate foliage and yellow plumes of *lady's bedstraw* and the little red tufted, green spheres of *salad burnet* favour these more calcium-rich soils. A few sites hold the powdery yellow pom-poms of *sulphur clover*, a plant whose British distribution is centred around the boulder clay geology of East Anglia, much as the *oxlip* inhabits the woodlands over a similar area.

Heathland exhibits a very different flora, consisting of plants unable to tolerate the lime-rich influence of the calcareous situation but possessing the means to deal with the paucity of nutrients in very acidic soils. The heathers are the most obvious visual distinction, their purple haze drifting among the *gorse* scrub a real summer delight. Three species of heather occur in Essex. The familiar *ling* is the most commonly encountered, although all are somewhat localised in occurrence given the general scarcity of their habitats.

The tiny pink flowers of *ling* are very different to their relations. *Bell heather* sports larger, bright pink urn-shaped flowers, the *cross-leaved heath* with a clutch of paler blooms clustered atop the stem. These are plants respectively of dry and wet heaths, the latter very scarce beyond the surviving areas of Epping Forest heathland. Rarely do all three inhabit the same locality, but at Tiptree Heath we are given such a privilege. In spite of the struggle to maintain the heathland habitats at Tiptree, this is a splendid piece of countryside, encompassing a mosaic of habitats. Fringed by woodland of *oak* and *birch*, the dry heath gives way to wetter areas and acid grassland. A stream bisects the heath, harbouring ferns and *liverworts* adding further vegetative variety to this fascinating site.

Of course, many of the plants we find at Tiptree Heath are characteristic of the heathland habitat in general. *Tormentil* scrambles among the shorter turf, littering the ground with four-petalled, yellow cinquefoil flowers. The diminutive *heath milkwort* peeks through the surrounding vegetation, little blue flowers adding a glint among the dark green foliage of the spreading heather. In the acid grasslands that comprise the heathland mosaic, species like *early hair-grass* and the *sweet vernal grass* are distinctive components of this community. The latter is one of the first to flower, their swathes of nodding heads providing a spring display that invariably goes unsung.

An interest in the taxing task of identifying the grasses and their allies can reward us with the discovery of uncommon plants such as *green-ribbed* and *pill sedges* as we delve into this rather more neglected sphere of botany. The grasses, rushes and sedges may lack the striking blooms of their floriferous counterparts, but the assorted plumes and sprays of feathery inflorescence possess a beauty of their own.

Surreptitious Bugs and Glorious Butterflies

Given the floral diversity of the grassland habitat, it is not surprising that among the vegetation we find a similarly rich variety of invertebrate life. Hidden among the tussocks and rising stems a host of small creatures live their lives in concealment but for the attentive investigation of the more inquisitive onlooker.

Flowers and foliage alike are predicated upon by feeding invertebrates. Closer examination of, say, the flower of an *ox-eye* or a *hogweed umbel* may reveal a mini-drama of life and death being enacted, where the consumer becomes the consumed, itself indeed the simple mechanics of life in this infinitely complex and perplexing entity we call nature.

Many and various are the bugs, beetles and flies that are attracted to feed on the flowers and the developing seeds of plants. Some are large enough to be observed without great difficulty. The pollen-feeding beetle *Oedemera nobilis* is a common insect and easily recognised by the metallic green, swollen thighs of the males. Nevertheless, many of the larger insects we are most likely to notice are predatory insectivores. The familiar red *soldier beetles* may be seen in number, particularly on the flowers of umbellifers, and *sailor beetles*, with black rather than red elytra (the hardened forewings typical of the *Coleoptera*) are equally as prolific. Bugs (*Hemiptera*) also hunt the meadow flowers. The *common flower bug* is one of the most abundant in Britain. These voracious little predators will even suck human blood if given the opportunity, a feature in common with their parasitic, bedbug relatives.

No wonder, then, that some vegetarian bugs stay within the relative concealment of the stems, like the very common *Stenodema laevigatum* and *Notostira elongata*. It is here that we can also find the familiar cuckoo-spit frothing around the stems. Not the saliva of the bird in the name, as many of us at some point in our childhood would like to have believed, but the protection afforded by adult *froghoppers* to the nymphs within. These insects possess a great ability for jumping, springing into the air when danger threatens. The handsome *red and black froghopper* launches itself to safety with an audible ping as it ejects itself from the platform of its leaf.

In spite of the undeniable benefits a diverse range of wild flowers will bring to the grassland invertebrate communities, it is the grasses themselves that are an especially important group of plants. They are incredibly productive plants in terms of the numbers of species that they support. *Cock's-foot*, for example, has been known to provide food for at least twenty different species of butterfly and larger moths, not to mention the numerous bugs, micro-moths and grasshoppers that feed widely on the range of different grasses on offer.

It is this latter group of insects that are one quintessential aspect of this quintessential habitat. It is the wall of sound generated by the unrelenting chorus of hundreds of 'singing' grasshoppers that surrounds you on entering into the vicinity of their grassy haven. Its pitch provides an aural quality to the equally insistent rays of the sun, the noise infiltrating your senses as much as the heat of high summer that washes in around you.

Among the seemingly constant drone, each species of grasshopper has its own song. They sing, or stridulate, by rubbing specially adapted stridulatory pegs situated on the hind femur against raised veins of the forewing. With the true crickets and bush-crickets, the two sets of wings are rubbed against each other to achieve a sound. To the trained ear the three-second long, sewing machine burst of the *meadow grasshopper* is quite distinct from the half-dozen or more, short chirps of the *field grasshopper*. There are, however, those who stay silent. The smaller *groundhopper* bears more than a strong resemblance to grasshoppers, but they lack the stridulatory organs of their relations.

Grasses support many species of *Lepidoptera*, insects that we all associate with that perfect summer scene of the whispering grasses graced by the dance of butterflies. They are dependent on the various species as their larval foodplants. The *meadow browns* that bounce above the sward originate from caterpillars that would have gorged themselves on *fescues* and *bents*, as would the *gatekeepers* that sun themselves on the bordering hedgerows and bramble scrub. In fact, all of the 'browns' feed on grasses, with both *fescue* and *bent* species featuring in the diet of practically all of them.

Few other browns are quite as widespread across the county's grasslands, although the *small heath* is an inconspicuous butterfly, perhaps eluding more regular observation with a propensity for keeping low among the grasses. *Ringlets* can be rather numerous at favoured sites and, similar to the *gatekeeper*, exhibit a liking for the shrubby fringes and also the semi-shade of the woodland edge. They are butterflies of simple beauty. Plain of wing, both upper and under, the rich dark brown coloration is broken only by a number of yellow-ringed black spots, centred by a glint of white. The *marbled white*, with their black and creamy white chequered markings echoed by the lattice of the underwing, is perhaps the most attractive of the browns and our most localised, generally regarded as being dependent on the presence of *red* and *sheep's fescue*. An insect often characteristic of the chalk and limestone grasslands of Southern England, they are something of a speciality of the south Essex grasslands, although an expansion in range over recent years may be taking them further into the county.

Along with the flutter of the *browns*, the buzz of *skippers* further enliven the meadows and pastures. Of the eight British species, three occur commonly in Essex. A fourth, the *grizzled skipper* hangs by a thread in its last county stronghold among the marvellous Langdon grasslands. These small, almost moth-like butterflies relish the hottest days of summer. The *large skipper* appears earliest, perhaps by the end of May. They are a species more prone to sheltered areas where they will often be found basking on fringing *bramble* scrub or the like.

Small and *Essex skippers* are more at home in the open grassland, darting their way among the grass stems, rarely rising much more than a metre above the ground. Come July and they are at their peak. Perhaps just for a single week will each individual insect be able to find a mate, but in the heat of the sun these short lives are filled with almost ceaseless activity. These are two very similar species who frequently fly together and they tease us with their 'will they land or won't they' antics as they move among the sward. On settling, we may have enough time to see the black tip to the underside of the antennae that would tell us we are looking at an *Essex skipper*. Those of the *small skipper* are entirely orange.

Of course, not all grassland butterflies are so closely tied to grasses. *Small coppers* lay their eggs on the various members of the dock family, particularly on *common* and *sheep's sorrel*. And no grassland scene can be complete without the vivid cerulean hues of *common blues*. Reflective scales refract the light from the sun – the brighter rays, the more dazzling the butterfly's coloration – but even on duller days their presence is always a brightening one. They number many species among their foodplants but always members of the *Fabacea* family, the pea flowers. Various clovers, *black medick* and *trefoils* can be used, but mainly *bird's-foot trefoil*. More often than not any blue butterfly flying in open grassland will be a *common blue*, the *holly blue* less likely to stray from the woodland or hedgerow edge.

The real identification challenge is provided by the *brown argus*, whose foodplant in Essex is most often likely to be the little pink-flowered *doves-foot cranesbill*. Neither sex is blue, but these little brown butterflies can easily be confused with female *common blues*. The *brown argus* often has a smaller, slightly neater demeanour, possessing an almost silvery quality as they flutter over the ground. They also lack the blue suffusion usually evident at the base of the female *common blue* upperwing. In common with a number of the *blues*, the *brown argus* in their larval stage enjoys an intriguing symbiosis with ants. The ants defend the caterpillars from would-be assailants and in return 'milk' them for the sweet secretion, which is then used to nourish the grubs of their own.

Not all day-flying *Lepidoptera* seen skimming across the fields will prove to be butterflies. Clovers and trefoils also comprise the habitat for certain diurnal moths that are as much a part of the Essex grassland scene as the butterflies. Stunning *six-spot burnets* zip about the place with direct level flight, more similar maybe to that of a bee than a moth. The caterpillars feed on *bird's-foot trefoil* and emerge from chrysalises slung on the stems of nearby grasses. They are one of the eager patrons of the *knapweed* flowers that adorn the grassy places. As the moths cluster on the flower heads, the striking red spots – set on dark metallic green wings – can be fully appreciated.

The *burnet companion* is much less gaudy; it is the yellow flash of the underwings that catches the eye, visible as they skip away from danger. The *latticed heath* also maintains a less conspicuous presence, but their filigree wings make for easy recognition.

The beauty among the grasses, however, will not always rest with delicate finery of butterflies and moths. There will always be those who will take a great deal of convincing of the various charms of the spider, but there is one that could sway even the biggest doubters. Among the taller grass the *wasp spider* casts its orb web among the stems. There are few more spectacular invertebrates at large in the British countryside, and certainly no spider more stunning. The centimetre-and-a-half-long body (of the female, the male is no more than a third her size) is coloured yellow, perhaps with a hint of creamy white, striped with black lines and with long banded legs they hang almost majestically from their web. Nationally they are scarce creatures and in Essex find themselves somewhere close to the northernmost edge of their range.

While the heathland habitat will invariably exhibit much overlap in the invertebrates commonly encountered there, its distinctive flora has inevitably resulted in the presence of certain rather more characteristic species; of the butterflies one in particular comes to mind. Throughout its range the *green hairstreak* is a butterfly of grassland and moor, as well as heath, colonies of each habitat exploiting different foodplants. On the fine heathland habitats of Danbury Common *gorse* and *broom* are the most widely used, where this localised species in Essex provides a rare treat while exploring the jumbled habitats of the common and the neighbouring Backwarden reserve. Rather in keeping with the *hairsteaks* in general, the *greens* are butterflies somewhat easily overlooked, but at least they spend most of their time around ground level, unlike their high-flying *purple* cousins. In flight the emerald green underside is offset by a brown upperwing, making them surprisingly difficult to track as they flutter among the vegetation, the hues of the former providing discrete coloration when at rest.

The most spectacular *Lepidopteran* frequently associated with heathland, however, has to be the splendid *emperor moth*. It is actually an insect of various habitats, taking a number of different foodplants, including the ubiquitous *bramble* and *hawthorn*. But a fondness for *heather* makes a heathland encounter with this spectacular moth a distinct possibility, all the more so as the males take to the wing during daylight hours. Even in flight he is unmistakable, the large eyespots in each of his four wings and the orange wash of the hindwings are easily discernable features. Other than the *hawk-moths* that will match and indeed dwarf the *emperor* for size, there is little opportunity for confusion, especially as the *hawks* are generally nocturnal anyway.

There is much less chance of seeing the female *emperor*. She is a nocturnal flyer, spending the day resting on vegetation, wafting out hormone signals to broadcast her presence to any males within her vicinity. The feathery antennae of the male can detect a female's scent from as far as two kilometres away. The larva, at least in the latter stages, are no less singular in appearance. From small black grubs they develop into handsome green caterpillars, almost the size of a little finger, dotted with yellow and red spots. The *emperor* has to be one of the finest of all British moths.

The heathland is alive with other insects. Where freshwater is present, such as the The Backwarden nature reserve, part of Danbury Common, a number of pools – relics of previous gravel extraction – support several species of dragonfly and damselfly. The classic *Odonata* of wet heaths are all but absent from Essex, but we can still enjoy the zip and dash of the commoner species as they hawk over the open spaces. And various creatures take advantage of the safety and shelter of the spiny foliage of the *gorse*. The *gorse shield bug*, one of a group of bugs who take their name from their supposed resemblance to a heraldic shield, may provide company for any *hairstreak* grubs.

The song of grasshoppers permeates the airspace, just as they do on their grassland retreats. As with the *Odonata*, none of the characteristic British heathland species occur in the county, the orthopteran hum being delivered by those species familiar from the wider countryside. Some, however, do find this habitat particularly to their liking. The combination of bare ground and low vegetation typical of the heath provides the perfect conditions for the non-singing *common groundhopper*. Feeding on moss and algae, they are equally happy in wet as they are in dry localities, so much so that those powerful hind legs prove just as useful for swimming as they are for jumping.

The heathland ground-dwellers lead an uncertain existence, though. Draped like veils among the low-growing plants, the extravagant constructions of *sheet-web spiders* adorn the late summer heath. The architect of such ingenious entrapment is the spider *Agelena labyrinthica*, one of only two European *sheet-webs* and the sole British representative. The spider waits concealed in a short, silken tunnel, set behind the expanse of the ensnaring sheet. The threads are not sticky, the webs instead equipped with a number of tripwires with which to entangle their prey, perhaps an unfortunate *groundhopper* springing itself haplessly into the web. No sooner does the spider detect any movement on the threads, it is racing across to grasp its prey, retreating back to its tubular recess to feed. Not everyone will be convinced of the charms of the spider itself, but we cannot fail to be impressed by their resourcefulness and eye for design.

RUSTLES AMONG THE HEDGEROWS

As we enter into a flowery meadow and allow ourselves to be absorbed by its mellow ambience of gentle urgency, it is often a luxuriant hedgerow or bordering scrub that frames the picture, giving us seclusion from whatever lies beyond, allowing our senses to concentrate fully on what surrounds us. And just as we are given an impression of concealment from what is without, these leafy and usually thorny havens provide the scene with the sweet sound of birdsong and the secreted movements of mammalian residents.

Needless to say, like the grasslands that they encompass, hedge and scrub is rich in invertebrate life. *Speckled* and *dark bush-crickets* add their own accompaniment to the orthopteran composition that rings out from among the sward. *Bramble* flowers will prove too tempting for the local butterflies; *meadow browns* are lured up from the meadow, taking nectar along with the ringlets and gatekeepers, not to mention the host of hoverflies, bees and others. Nevertheless, the full extent of the huge productivity of the scrubby habitats is barely done justice by the nectaring butterflies that flutter around the *bramble* blossom. The likes of *hawthorn* and *blackthorn* can support a huge diversity of invertebrates, well over three hundred in the case of the former. This includes a great many moths, in particular the *geometers*, one of the larger moth families. Of the many, the *brimstone moth* is one of those that are more likely to attract casual attention with its long flight season, from April to October, and bright yellow colour. Their caterpillars, however, are the masters of disguise. They are dull grey-brown in colour, and standing themselves upright on the prolegs at the back end of the body (caterpillars only have six legs, just like any other insect, the stumps at the back providing a means of keeping a firm hold of the foodplant when feeding) they assume the appearance of a twig. This is a strategy employed by a number of other *geometer* moths.

It is this invertebrate abundance, along with the thorny shelter afforded, which makes hedgerow and scrub such an attractive proposition for small birds. With the coming of spring they receive the arrival of migrants returning from Africa. The shrubs will once more hide the skulk of *whitethroats*, betrayed perhaps by their scratchy warbled tones. Their song is certainly as varied as the closely related *blackcap*, but is somewhat lacking in the tuneful liquidity of the latter. That is not to say that the sight and sound of the *whitethroat* is not as keenly anticipated after a long winter. Theirs is a cheerful presence, another clue to the increase in activity and productivity as the climate warms with the winter forgotten. As self-effacing as one might expect from a warbler, an eager male might break from his hidden perch to deliver his song on a descending display flight. At rest atop a bush, the rich chestnut of their wings can be seen more clearly, as can the eponymous white throat. But their frustrating preference for deep cover is nothing compared to the *lesser whitethroat*, barely smaller than the name might suggest and much greyer. They are a bird almost as widespread, although much less numerous in Essex than their cousin and one that is so often overlooked.

We are still more likely to catch sight of a *lesser whitethroat* than the small mammals that inhabit the hedgerows and grassland. A hovering *kestrel*, quivering wings at contrast to head held dead still and eyes transfixed on the ground below, will bear testament to the *field voles* that scurry among the grass. As is the *barn owl*, whose magnificent pale visage, silently quartering the open countryside, will always deliver a tingle of excitement as they float ethereally through the fading light of dusk. Unlike the *bank vole*, *field voles* are poor climbers and, spending most of their time on the ground nibbling at grass stems, they are able to muster a fair burst of speed if so required. Such pace can make the difference between life and death for the *field vole*. In addition to the threat from above, there are voracious predators on the ground to contend with. The *weasel* is a diminutive hunter with a justifiably fearsome reputation as a predator of small mammals, of which voles are an important part of their diet. They are lithe and agile pursuers, able to track their prey into their own burrows if necessary. Such abilities require a great deal of energy and *weasels* need to eat daily to sustain themselves.

The small mammal contingent of the heathland environment may be presented with a different threat. The *adder* is a widespread and resilient reptile. They are creatures of various kinds of open countryside, but the presence of bare sunny ground alongside deep cover, so typical of this habitat, is very much to their liking. They are rather more easily observed here than among the tall grassy places that they will also frequent, especially in the spring when they are keen to make full use of the still increasing intensity of the early vernal sunshine. The brown zig-zag markings of the female makes for a rather cryptic coloration, but the silver black pattern of the male is one of striking and beautiful contrast.

And while the *weasel* relies on its boundless energy to chase down its prey, the *adder* takes a more surreptitious approach based on guile and surprise. Tasting the air for scent with that constantly flicking tongue and feeling for vibrations on the ground, the *adder* patiently tracks its prey. In spite of its slow, almost lazy progress over the ground, its reflexes when administering a fatal bite to an unsuspecting victim are lightning fast. A painful bite to a human is a lethal dose to voles and mice, or indeed the *common lizards* that also find good living on the copious *wolf spiders* and the like that teem on the sun-baked ground. While the adults tackle these larger animals, the exact miniatures that are their young cut their teeth on more manageable invertebrate prey. So very different is their strategy to their mammalian counterparts, but no less admirable is the efficiency of their pursuit.

Along the field edges, *common shrews* share the hidden world of the deep grass. A loud squeak from within the vegetation is the most frequent evidence of their presence beyond the stare of human eyes. They are intolerant little beasts and this is the sound of an inevitable show of aggression as two shrews confront each other upon a chance meeting. These are remarkable little creatures. They need to consume huge quantities of food just to stay alive, perhaps as much as ninety per cent of their own bodyweight every day – maybe even two hundred per cent for females with a litter of half-a-dozen milk-hungry mouths to feed – yet they do not hibernate, toughing out the winter months. Thus, they are ravenous consumers of slugs, snails, earthworms and a variety of other invertebrate prey. Perhaps the winter wildflower meadow is not quite the lifeless place it may at first appear.

It is only really the *rabbit* that ensures regular mammal sightings, the *grey squirrel* of the open countryside in terms of their obviousness in their given habitats. Having arrived with the Normans in the 12th century, they must surely now be regarded as honorary native. Where populations are large enough they can be pests, munching their way through crops and newly planted trees and shrubs. But their nibbling can add variety to grassland communities. Indeed, following the introduction of myxomatosis in the 1950s, as a controlling measure of burgeoning *rabbit* populations, important herb-rich grasslands in Southern England fell into neglect and ruin, succumbing to the encroachment of scrub and the loss of their valuable floral assemblages.

In Essex, *rabbit* predators are few and far between, and even though myxomatosis may have succeeded in eradicating them from some of their more marginal haunts, they thrive across the county. The *buzzard*, a well-known hunter of rabbits, is a bird rare (but increasing) to the area and in many places the *red fox* is their only real threat. Their classic predator is the *stoat*, as finely honed a consumer of *rabbits* as its smaller cousin the *weasel* is of mice and voles. They will happily tackle prey as big as themselves, such is their predatory skill and tenacity. They are relentless in their pursuit of their quarry, hounding them down oblivious even to a bemused and very fortunate human onlooker. For the most part though, this is a shy and scarcely seen animal and perhaps a declining one in Essex, a sighting of which is always something rather special.

GRASSLAND AND HEATH IN ESSEX

1. THE BACKWARDEN
(Explorer 183, Grid Reference 781 041)
Separated from Danbury Common by a road, this 12ha site is managed by The Essex Wildlife Trust. A great variety of habitats in a limited area. Small areas of heathland provides excellent reptile habitat, with *adders* regularly seen. The *green hairstreak* also occurs.

2. DANBURY COMMON
(Exp 183, GR 781 041)
At 87ha, this National Trust property incorporates one the largest areas of heathland in Essex. Woodland and scrub is full of birdsong in spring with the arrival of *nightingales* and *warblers*. Interesting insects include *green hairstreaks* and the rare *rosy marbled moth*.

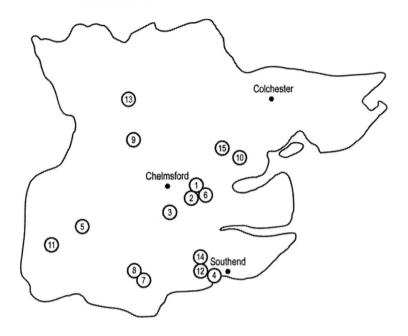

3. GALLEYWOOD COMMON
    (Exp 183, GR 704 025)

A 24ha area of common land that still contains a small area of heathland. The songs of *willow warblers* ring out among the surrounding woodland in the spring, and ponds created by gravel extraction provide good foraging for bats.

4. HADLEIGH CASTLE COUNTRY PARK
    (Exp 175, GR 799 870)

A huge variety of habitats includes extensive areas of cattle grazed grassland and scrub alive with nesting birds. Many wildflowers can be found including, *grass vetchling, agrimony* and *common centuary*. The slopes of Belton Hills (Exp 175, GR 825 860) have *spiny restharrow* and the scarce *bythinian vetch*. An excellent butterfly site. *White-letter hairstreak, brown argus, marbled white* and regular *clouded yellow* are among the more unusual.

5. HAWKSMERE SPRINGS
    (Exp 175, GR 508 993)

This small area of unimproved pasture harbours a wealth of wildflowers. *Cowslips* are one species providing spring colour, stands of *meadowsweet* proliferating later in the season. Damper areas add variety with the likes of *hard rush* and *bugle*.

6. HITCHCOCK'S MEADOWS
   (Exp 183, GR 788 049)

A wonderfully rich area of ancient pastureland adjoining the eastern edge of Danbury Common. A very diverse flora includes *green-winged orchid*, the scarce *autumn lady's tresses* and *heath dog violets*. The *speckled yellow moth* feeds on the *wood sage* that abounds.

7. HORNDON MEADOW
   (Exp 175, GR 672 851)

A tiny 1ha remnant of unimproved hay meadow containing an impressive array of wildflowers, among them a fine spring showing of *green-winged orchid* and *yellow rattle*.

8. LANGDON

The Essex Wildlife Trust Landgon Nature Reserve (Exp 175, GR 659 874) and Langdon Hills Country Park (Exp 175, GR 697 861) cover a combined area of some 344ha. Both areas contain important grassland habitats. Unimproved grassland comprises significant areas of the splendid patchwork of habitats at the Langdon Nature Reserve. It is fine area for butterflies and is the last remaining Essex location for the *grizzled skipper*.

9. ONSLOW GREEN
   (Exp 183, GR 654 183)

This 1ha nature reserve is in fact a village green, managed by the Essex Wildlife Trust. Various interesting plants grow here, including the scarce *sulphur clover*. A large pond is a haven for dragonflies.

10. OXLEY MEADOW
   (Exp 184, GR 918 149)

The May display of *meadow buttercup* and *green-winged orchid* is breathtaking, a time when *orange tip* butterflies flutter along the luxuriant hedgerows. *Adder's-tongue fern* is much less conspicuous but nonetheless numerous.

11. RODING VALLEY MEADOWS
   (Exp 175, GR 430 943)

This 63ha Essex Wildlife Trust reserve comprises the largest area of traditional hay meadow in the county. The meadow flowers include, in the damper areas, the lovely *southern marsh orchid*. The winding River Roding delineates the western boundary of the reserve, giving added interest with the opportunity of seeing *kingfisher* and *banded demoiselle*.

12. SHIPWRIGHTS WOOD
   (Exp 175, GR 795 871)

Abutting this attractive woodland is a small flower-rich meadow. A very interesting flora includes *common spotted orchid, hairy St John's-wort, musk mallow* and *wild carrot*.

13. SWEETINGS MEADOW
   (Exp 195, GR 632 285)

One of the few surviving traditional boulder-clay hay meadows. A rich flora includes *bee* and *pyramidal orchids*.

14. THUNDERSLEY COMMON
   (Exp 175, GR 798 896)

This 14ha piece of common land contains woodland, acid grassland and small area of heath. *Cross-leaved heath* grows alongside the dominant *ling* and *gorse* on the heath, while *green-ribbed sedge* is among some unusual grassland plants.

15. TIPTREE HEATH
   (Exp 184, GR 883 146)

An immensely interesting area comprised of a mosaic of habitats. Wet and dry heath, acid grassland and secondary woodland are all present, along with streams and ponds. In spring the heath is alive with birdsong, including *nightingale* and *garden warbler*. *Common lizards* are also present.

CHAPTER FIVE

Essex's Unsung Wetlands

FROM MARSHY RIVERSIDES TO TWINKLING LAKES

It is arguably the famous coastal wetlands of Essex that puts the county on the national map, in terms of its ecological and conservation significance: the freshwater wetlands of the interior, with some exceptions, the subject of rather less eulogising. This is perhaps justified to a certain extent: the great spread of the Norfolk Broads rather steals the show on this score. But away from the spotlight this county contains many inland wetlands worthy of celebration, with winding rivers, the open water of lakes and their accompanying marshy habitats comprising a crucial strand in the unsung tapestry of wild Essex.

There are a number of significant river systems that wend their way across the Essex countryside. Several originate in the higher country to the north. The Chelmer and the Pant via the River Blackwater flow down from the northwesterly quarter of the county, letting into the Chelmer and Blackwater Navigation on its way to the coast. The Colne maintains a more west-east direction before arcing down through Colchester, its estuary merging with the Blackwater at Mersea Island.

And along the way they gain the waters from a series of lesser rivers and brooks. The Roman River cuts into the Colne opposite Wivenhoe, and the River Can flows into the Chelmer at Chelmsford – not before it has been joined itself by the Wid further upstream. By the time the Chelmer gains the water of the River Ter near Utling, it has assumed the moniker of the canalised Chelmer and Blackwater Navigation. With the Brain merging upstream at Witham, the River Blackwater proper meets the early tidal waters of the Chelmer just west of Maldon, while the Navigation carries its freshwater through the last few kilometres to the gape of the Blackwater Estuary.

To the south, the courses of the Crouch and Roach are rather dominated by the tidal reaches of their long snaking estuaries, that in effect provide a delving inland protrusion of the coastline, where *bladder wrack* and *oystercatchers* – and not the *bulrush* and *moorhen* – are the order of the day. As the Crouch heads south from its source near Billericay, its presence in the landscape is inconspicuous, to the extent that one would scarcely know it was there but for the use of a map. A mere stream at this point, its trickling waters are often well hidden by scrub and shading trees. Little water-life is evident to the naked eye in the youthful river, but for the surface skating *water crickets* that favour such conditions. Struggling its way through Wickford, one can almost imagine a sense of relief as it winds out towards Battlesbridge and the open country of its estuary beyond. Also in the southern reaches of Essex, and draining into the Thames, are a number of tributaries arising from more central parts of the county, including the River Roding, the Ingrebourne River, and Mar Dyke.

Two more rivers have a significant bearing on the Essex landscape, providing a large part of the county border. The Stour separates Essex and Suffolk along a large section, marking as it does the border between the two counties – the River Stort via the River Lea to the east doing much the same between Essex and Hertfordshire.

These ribbons of watery sanctuary provide us with some of the most restful scenery in the county, as they thread their way through the relative bleakness of an often heavily cultivated environment. They are usually well concealed in the flat or gently sloping landscapes in which they tend to be found, but we can often trace their passage by the silvery-green foliage of the bankside *willows* that provide an above-ground clue to their low-lying presence. In this respect, rivers and even narrow streams and brooks play a hugely important role in the ecology of the Essex countryside. Not only for their aquatic habitats are they important, but also the adjacent fringes of scrub, hedgerow and occasional bankside woodland that create linear oases for many plants and animals not necessarily directly associated with aquatic ecosystems.

This fact is ably illustrated by the Mar Dyke as it inches sluggishly through the enticingly named, but long-ago drained and cultivated Bulphan and Orsett Fens. Its first impression is one of being pleasant if unspectacular. But as the arable fields approach the line of the dyke, their progress is halted by a sharp drop down to the bank of the waterway, leaving a broad strip of uncultivated land where wildlife can thrive. *Meadow browns* gather to feed on the stands of *mayweed* that grows along field edge, skimming among the rough grass with other butterflies like *small heath, skippers* or even *ringlet*, while *whitethroat, yellowhammer* and *linnet* call from the waterside scrub. On reflection, the dyke seems a little less unremarkable than it might have seemed on arrival.

There is little that can match the tranquility of a lowland river as it winds its way lazily towards the sea, generating as it goes an air of contentment with its unwavering destiny. The splendid countryside of the wonderful Dedham Vale and the River Stour speaks for itself. Here lies the only officially recognised Area of Natural Beauty in Essex. The area has a reputation that has undoubtedly been aided by its ties with the famous artist John Constable at Flatford Mill, but such lovely countryside would surely have achieved national acclaim without such publicity. Elsewhere, the rivers of Essex deliver further, less well-known delights. In hidden nooks, secret stretches of paradise await.

As the Roman River flows just south of Colchester, its breadth barely exceeds a great deal more than jumping distance, much like the youthful stretches of our more major rivers, well upstream of their estuarine destinations. But as it runs through the Essex Wildlife Trust reserve at Layer-de-la-Haye it does not need to be some broad sweeping watercourse to make its presence felt among its cool and verdant surrounds. Riverine woodland of *alder* and *willow* echoes with birdsong and creates dappled shade on the bending river below. This airy, cool canopy is a joy on the balmy spring and summer days, the leaves soaking up the heat of the sun while we take temperate relief below. The rich alluvial soil grows thick with *nettle* and *meadowsweet*, the realm of numerous tiny beasts – beetle, bug, spider and snail, or mayflies taking leave of their fleeting experience of life on the wing.

Against this lush green backdrop, the shimmering blue of *beautiful* and *banded demoiselles* – catching the occasional flicker of sunlight through canopy – take on an enhanced iridescence. In instances where the banks are less sheltered than one may find elsewhere, little of the reassuring seclusion is lost. Marginal plants grow strong in the sun – *bulrush, reedmace* and *iris* standing tall above the pads of *yellow water-lily* that float on the surface.

The more spacious water of the Chelmer and the Chelmer and Blackwater Navigation provides an alternative to the intimacy of these less voluminous rivers. Although less meandering, particularly along the canalised navigation, the broader waters bend satisfyingly through the landscape. This is a marvellous river to ramble beside. Whereas the beautiful environs of other rivers, like the Colne, Blackwater or Stour, tantalise us with only broken stretches of parallel footpaths, and where roads cross their course, here we can walk a towpath that extends virtually unbroken from Chelmsford to Maldon. The riparian *willows* that arch elegantly over the broad sweep of the river have a less dominating influence, never completely shading the water. Moisture-loving wildflowers flourish among the bankside vegetation, like the glorious spikes of *purple loosestrife* that stand proudly among the tangle of foliage. The clear waters can yield more easily obtained views of the resident fish than perhaps elsewhere, such as the predatory *perch* lurking among the fringing *reedmace*.

Many a long hour can be spent by the river; peering into the depths for a glimpse of the teeming fish, taking in the comings and goings of the numerous creatures that are drawn in, perhaps by something of the same magnetism that has captivated us. But to view the scene from within its midst – from the surface of the water itself, gives a different perspective. Even though, in our rowing boat we may move so deliberately across the water, compared to the effortless drift and dash of the damselflies and dragonflies that adorn the marginal vegetation and floating lilies we may gain some sense of participation. Without the noise of a motor to break the whisper of the wind among the towering *alder* boughs and riverside *willows*, or the smell of exhaust fumes to overpower the subtle scents that hint of the lushness that surrounds, the colourful riparian residents seem most ready to accept our presence in their domain.

The aquatic environment would have once extended far beyond the riverbank. As they twisted their way through the landscape, the winter rains would have caused the rivers to inundate the flood meadows along the way, their subsequent drying and grazing accommodating rich meadow swards. Marshes would have accompanied the bends of the river, land never fully beyond its moistening influence.

Alas, such habitats now only survive in Essex as fragments. Marshes have been drained for agriculture and floodplains given over to development. Their loss has been quite staggering. Think of a great marshland that once filled the low country on the Thames floodplain, covering thousands upon thousands of square hectares, and then consider the mere thirteen hectares of Cranham Marsh, a splendid little nature reserve on the urban fringe of metropolitan Essex and a rare surviving relic of the south Essex marshlands. But within the remnants that remain dotted around the county we can still find intact the magic and luxuriance of these rich and fertile habitats.

Few significant areas of freshwater marshland remain. Notably there is the reserve at Cranham, although this area is not as wet as it used to be, and nine hectares of marshland habitat comprising the splendid little Sawbridgeworth Marsh Reserve, a fair chunk of which actually lies in Hertfordshire, but straddling the border as it does, it was purchased jointly by the two respective Wildlife Trusts. But one of the most important areas is the seventy-five hectares of marshland that fills the shallow valley of the River Ingrebourne, an area of wonderful wildlife habitat and so close to the clutter of metropolitan Essex.

Ours aren't the expansive areas of the Somerset Levels or the Norfolk Broads, but the essence of their former glories oozes within these retracted bastions. Once within their bounds they are places where the unseen rhythm of life can almost be felt. Not quite like the audible buzz of the summer meadow, but more subliminal. Sure enough, the *bush-crickets* and *grasshoppers* sing their songs, but their chorus, along with the rring *sedge warblers* and reeling *grasshopper warblers*, provides a kind of sonorous veneer to the depth within. We may have to pause, to listen intently; where one moment there was just the rustle of the breeze through the plethora of sedges, rushes and damp-loving grasses, the next there is an added richness to the sound elevated into our consciousness. One could easily be describing the unseen diversity of the ancient wood or indeed the heat-fuelled flourish of the wildflower meadow. These are personal experiences that can and should be attributed to whatever place the individual deems appropriate to choose and should never be restricted to any one. Nevertheless, for this author such celebratory words flow easily with these habitats in mind, where the air can be thick with existence.

An early June visit to Sawbridgeworth Marsh should be all the convincing one would need. With the spring well underway, the verdant stands of *reed, sedge* and *willowherb* give physicality to the plenty of the season. In places, the marsh is rarely free of water, elsewhere damp meadowland prevails. Here and there the opulent green of the tall vegetation of fen and marsh is interrupted by the stunning pink-purple spikes of *southern marsh orchid.* All the while the place teems with insect life, made most obvious by the dragonflies and damselflies that breed in the open water of the ditches and the River Stort that skirts the western edge of the nature reserve, not forgetting the chatter and warble of the numerous but skulking small birds that take their fill of the riches of the marsh. Scarcely though, can an all-too-familiar tale of destruction be tempered with one of regeneration.

But this does tell part of the story of wetlands in Essex. So rarely our modern-day exploitation of natural resources ends in anything but damage to local habitats and the loss of its wildlife, however in some areas this is proving to be the case. For decades, gravel has been extracted from all over the county. Over time the scars of industry heal, the deep depressions become filled with water and the bare banks invaded by pioneering plants. Where the machines of industry have long departed and the recovery for all intents and purposes complete, we may then bear witness to nature's amazing propensity for regeneration and recovery if allowed the time to do so. Not since the 1960s has the landscape at the Fingringhoe Wick nature reserve been shaped in this way, and the lake here has the appearance of a feature almost as permanent as the Colne Estuary alongside which the reserve is situated.

Essex has no natural lakes, but the appearance of these manmade bodies of water fits seamlessly, at least after a period of time, into the landscape. As the vegetation returns it serves to blur the harshness of the hard edges left by uncompromising machines. From bare banks through *bramble* scrub to *willow* carr woodland, the transformation can be remarkable. In places, namely at Stanford Warren, they have come to harbour extensive reedbeds. Some pits are still being worked, representing the very beginning of the process.

Elsewhere, worked out pits have been widely preserved as fishing lakes; others feature significantly among the county's nature reserves. Part of a complex just north of Maldon, the Essex Wildlife Trust owns a series of flooded pits comprising their Chigborough Lakes reserve. The numerous fishing lakes represent an aesthetically beneficial form of land use, or perhaps that should be water use, and one not without further benefits for wildlife, but those waters set aside as areas specifically for wildlife present a rather different ambience. Where the banks on one might be kept clear for the comfort anglers, on the other they will be left to the rambling *brambles* and thirsty *willows*. It is this dense barrier that on the one hand frustrates, where we hear the sounds of the wildlife within but struggle to gain a view.

But the needs of human visitors will always be accommodated where appropriate. An opening reveals the peaceful waters, framed by the leafy surrounds that initially denied us, but that also offers the seclusion sought after by the waterfowl – *pochard, grebe* and *coot*, whose wake is all that disturbs the gently rippling surface.

But it is not our desire for that which lays underground that generates the most expansive single areas of open water, but the basic needs of a thirsty population. The reservoirs of Abberton and Hanningfield dwarf anything created by the aggregates industry, with the notable exception of the vast and wildlife-rich complex of old gravel workings that now comprise the Lee Valley Regional Park. Covering an area of some four hundred and eighty hectares, Abberton is the larger of the two, with the smaller Hanningfield Reservoir occupying an area of a mere three hundred and sixty hectares. With the hard concrete banks, only intermittently smothered by fringing vegetation, they lack something of the warmth and continuity in the landscape of the reclaimed gravel workings, but they are nevertheless peaceful and spacious places that provide a dramatic punctuation to the rolling green, rural landscapes among which they sit.

The signs of human construction are never far away, but here and there marshy fringes do occur, allowing nature to soften the contrived edge. This is where passing waders might stop over to pick along the muddy edge or where areas of reed may become established, ensuring the chatter of *reed warblers* beneath the inevitable *goat willow* – a bolt hole for those waterbirds reluctant to stray too far from cover.

Along much of its western half, Hanningfield is embraced by bordering woodland, serving to soften the harshness of the encircling band of concrete. Much is plantation, but to the south the conifers are well mixed with hardwoods. Some parts are of ancient origin. From *grebes* and *gadwall* to *goldcrest* and *great spotted woodpeckers*, the wooded shore offers a varied wildlife experience. This combination of open water and woodland creates something of a lakeland feel, the vision of the burnished shades of a sunset sky spreading above the reflective waters and the darkening hues of the lakeside forest a rather unlikely vista in Essex. Even though the wooded bounds are rarely broader than a couple of hundred metres, it is easy to imagine a sprawling woodland stretching away into the countryside. A touch of fantasy maybe, but the wildlife of the woods is as rich and rewarding as that of the water. Words more apt for another chapter perhaps.

Despite their inherent artificiality, the county's major reservoirs rank highly among the birding fraternity, including to a lesser extent the much smaller but attractive Ardleigh Reservoir near Colchester. Abberton in particular has developed a justifiable reputation as one of Britain's best birdwatching spots. Rarities are frequent and scarce birds are regular, but whether a birdwatcher or not, the winter spectacle here is one that can be enjoyed on many different levels. The spring and summertime have their charms. There is the rather unusual sight of a colony of tree-nesting *cormorants*, the summer moult of hundreds of *mute swans*, and the stream of passage waders that pass through each autumn.

But as the various species of waterfowl descend on British shores to enjoy the relative mildness of our winter, Abberton really comes into its own. Counts of *mallard, teal, wigeon, pochard* and *tufted duck* will collectively run into many thousands, along with similarly vast congregations of *coot,* geese and gulls. And all this before we even attempt to pick out the rarer ducks and *grebes* that always put in an appearance. The chatter and babble of the scores of bustling birds is ceaseless. While an icy January wind can positively tear across the open water, the spreading rafts of bobbing heads across the lapping surface makes for warming sight, one that is always worth braving the plummeting winter temperatures, the very climate that will do much to further enhance a most seasonal scene.

The freshwater habitats of Essex thus paint a picture of variety and profusion. They can never, even the vast reservoirs, match the coastal wetlands for sweeping scenery and massive expanse. Their riches are instead scattered about the county – gravel pits here, a reservoir there, and the network of rivers and other waterways, too numerous to mention, that play such an important part in providing connectivity for the wild places that would otherwise exist in total isolation, as indeed many still do. And all this without mention of the numerous ponds that reside among all the habitats mentioned in this book: in woods and among grasslands, and of course those installed into hundreds of Essex back gardens.

Within this category some are of particular acclaim. Among its wonderful opportunities for wildlife the dozens of ponds dotted around the great Epping Forest are something of a rather distinctive feature. Indeed, the forest's wetland habitats comprise one the best dragonfly sites in the county. And of the humble garden pond, these are a vital wildlife resource never to be underestimated. Without them, how much more scarce would some of our familiar amphibians have become were they left solely to survive in the diminishing wetlands of the wider countryside?

We are fortunate also that as part of the bigger picture the destruction of the past has in some way been offset by the creation of new habitats. These modern wetlands are unlikely, however, to match the ecological richness of those that over centuries developed the complex interactions and wildlife communities that made their agonising loss so tragic, but at least for a change we can see the human exploitation of natural resources result in something positive for the other beings who must suffer our company. With the careful management of these new treasures, who knows what we can create for future generations. Perhaps eventually something that will begin to resemble more closely that which we have previously lost.

WETLAND WILDLIFE: A WORLD OF VARIETY

With the freshwater wetland represented in so many guises, each facet offers its own unique quality. Certain dragonflies, for example, will be attracted to the bare banks of a newly formed gravel pit, favouring this situation to the well-vegetated environs preferred by others, and while many species will inhabit various types of standing water, some require the flow of the stream or river. There are those aquatic insects that love for nothing better than to lurk in murk of a muddy bottom pond, others prefer a more stable base. Some plants are not able to establish themselves where there is the current of flowing water and species that will tolerate the varying degrees of wet and dry — a similar story to the life on the ever dynamic estuary, but rather less taxing for the organisms in question. It is such influential factors as these that present the wetland habitats in their various forms as such vibrant, varied and even surprising places to explore.

THE VERDANT CELEBRATION

One of the most appealing aspects of wetland flora is its lushness. The plants that are adapted to the variously wet conditions, be it a damp grassland typified by temporary inundation, a soggy spring-fed marsh or a purely aquatic habitat, their presence is rarely anything less than copious. A small pond might be thick with *hornwort*, its foliage alive with aquatic invertebrates and wriggling newts that we may only glimpse as they come to the surface for air, the muddy banks littered with the blue and yellow of *water forget-me-not* and *lesser spearwort*. As a river flows, *reed-mace* – not the *bulrush* as it is so often mislabelled – creeps tentatively into the moving water. Higher up on the bank the stands of *willowherb* might deny us unbroken observation, leaving us keen for the next unhindered view. It is the *yellow water-lily* that is most visible further towards the midstream – blooms for decoration, leaves for basking damselflies.

As the land surrounding the old gravel pits marches on through its succession back to woodland, it is the visage of the *willow* reflected in the shimmering waters, towering above the fringing reed and herbaceous plants that dominates the scene. And then there are the dense swathes of *rush* and *sedge* that rise from the wet marshland, broken by weed-filled ditches. Water is a necessity for all survival, an abundance of which is blatantly celebrated by the verdant wetland flora.

In those purely aquatic situations – that is the ponds, lakes and rivers where inundation is, generally speaking, a permanent feature – it is among the waters of shallow ponds that the richest assemblages of flowering plants are to be found. From the mass of submerged weed that will flourish in a healthy pond and the floating mat of *duckweed, water-plantain* may issue from the water, culminating in an elegant, open spike of small pink-white flowers. The plantain-like foliage bears only a superficial resemblance to their unrelated terrestrial namesakes.

The delightful little *water-violet*, its own flowering stem adorned with whorls of pretty pink blooms, is a rather scarcer sight in Essex. Some ponds may be decorated by *water-crowfoot*, aquatic members of the buttercup family, dozens of white flowers scattered across the surface, from a distance looking like the petals of fallen cherry blossom. With a number of similar species, there is a *crowfoot* for all occasions: still, moving or even brackish water. In bloom these are not difficult plants to spot, the challenge being that of distinguishing which one you have found. Start with the *common water-crowfoot* and work from there.

On larger water bodies, rafts of *water-lily* are given the space to provide a colourful spectacle. The landscaped grounds of the Danbury Lakes Country Park might struggle to compete for the attention of the naturist drawn to the riches of wonderful woods and heathland nearby, but the summer show of *white water-lily* can be splendid. And besides, the park certainly is not without its broader wildlife interest. The other native, the *yellow water-lily*, although also a species of still waters is often encountered as a plant of slow-moving rivers. The bright yellow, compact inflorescence is rather less showy than the striking mass of white petals of their relative, but theirs is a more subtle appeal as the curve of the pads edge their way in from the slacker waters nearer the bank. Yet to complete their journey from the depths of perhaps more than a metre, the emerging leaves visible beneath the surface yield gently to the flow of the water. Viewed from above they create a pleasing collage of merging greens and blues, softened shades provided by the river depths and reflected hues of the sky above.

At the pond edge a greater diversity of plants can be found, where those unable to tolerate the deeper waters can thrive. Indeed, as we move up the slope from the depths towards dry land a level of zonation becomes evident, although certainly not as profound as that associated with the flora of the coast and estuary. Of those that prevail in this area of transition, the magnificent *yellow iris* is arguably the most beautiful. The exquisite architecture of any iris flower can match those of the orchids, perhaps not in terms of ingenuity of design, but definitely for their pure aesthetic splendour.

But let this not detract from the contribution of other contingents of lesser stature. The yellow bloom of the *marsh marigold* is no less vivid than that of the iris, their early spring colour all the more vibrant with the drab days of winter still fresh in the mind. *Water forget-me-not* is a common plant of Essex ponds, and riversides for that matter, where their sprinkling of pale blue flowers mingle delicately with more visually robust foliage of mixed rushes and sedges. Of the rushes it is the *soft rush* that will be most common, round leaved and less domineering than their Carex counterpart, the *pendulous sedge*.

Most definitely not a plant for the small garden pond this common sedge will form substantial clumps on the waterside. But for their familiarity, they might be regarded in higher esteem, for it is a fine plant, with its eruption of dark green leaves and gracefully drooping inflorescence that lends them half of their name. The yellow buttercup of *lesser spearwort* is commonly encountered, as is the white haze of the massed tiny flowers of *marsh bedstraw*, plants of wider tolerance to the drying out of the soil. *Water mint* can occur in local abundance, scrambling around the marshy edge, suffusing the air with the fresh scent of their leaves, packed purple flower heads offering a popular source of nectar for bees and butterflies.

Those plants that begin to appear as the influence of the water lessens will often be those that also fringe the riverbanks, a habitat that can actually become very dry come the summer. Often a fertile and competitive environment, it helps to be of robust build to succeed on the riverside. Stands of *great willowherb* can occur in quantity and is a plant common to all kinds of damp habitats. Less ubiquitous is the *purple loosestrife*, but with long, gorgeous pink flower spikes, supported perhaps a metre of the ground, they are difficult to overlook.

Away from the immediate vicinity of the permanent water bodies the floral array will be similarly diverse. In the river valleys, pieces of marsh and fen survive and we might find areas of floodplain that have escaped the infilling of urban development.

The distinction between the marsh and fen is on the face of it a subtle one. Fen vegetation develops in the presence of nutrient rich, non-acidic water, and grows out of a bed of peat. Marshes lie directly over regular soil where the rich layer of organic matter is absent, thus their floral communities tend to be less diverse.

In practice, though, the species present will be largely similar and will invariably harbour some of the species familiar from the waterside habitats. Moisture-loving sedges, rushes and grasses, often of frustrating similarity to their kin, form a lush swathe of green. Many of the flowers of pond and lakeside might be encountered, along with the beautiful spikes of *southern marsh orchids* that provide striking interruption to this verdant backcloth. Where the vegetation grows tall, wildflowers need to be of similar proportions. The aromatic scent of *meadowsweet* may reach the nostrils before their fluffy white flower heads catch the eye, and at well over a metre in height, stands of *hemp-agrimony* will tower over most other herbaceous plants, umbels of pink pom-poms well attended by nectar hungry insects.

The dykes and ditches that bisect the marshlands may seem choked and stagnant, but can in fact harbour much interest and variety that might otherwise be overlooked. Flowering *crowfoots* are conspicuous but the varied thread-like and broad leaves of pondweeds rather less so. The *broad-leaved pondweed* is a plant of wide tastes, found in various types of still or slow-moving water, as is the filamentous-leaved *fen pondweed*.

Wherever we find the niches among the wetland habitats, their flora is rarely sparse.

A WORLD OF INVENTION

Copious vegetation sparks a compelling assemblage of insects and other invertebrates. Some will dazzle us, others will intrigue us, but always they will engender curious fascination. Of course, many of the creatures that flit and scurry among and around the varied wetland habitats are entirely terrestrial, attracted by the prolificacy of the plant life, but there will of course always be those that provide peculiarity to their habitats.

As with the flora, the obviously unique environment of a wholly aquatic habitat demands a high level of specialisation from its invertebrate inhabitants, and because of this engenders its own unique fascination. The amazing array of freshwater invertebrates embodies all of the enigmatic appeal that attracts us so strongly to the heaving wetland habitats. As we stare into the depths we are confronted by another world. Peering into the cool, clear water, through the break among the weed or beneath the reflected boughs of the riverside trees, the fleeting glimpses that we gain of the denizens below triggers that childlike fascination that might have captivated us in our youth, when you almost felt that you could slide in among the weedy labyrinth and explore at first hand the remarkable creatures within. These are feelings that thankfully stay with us and help to explain that great attraction that the aquatic environment has. Is it not almost impossible to walk past any kind of water body without pausing for a closer look?

The many invertebrates in their different guises are well represented. Water snails can be extremely numerous. On close observation, even such humble creatures have their own finery, with the spiral shell of the *pond snail*, shorter in the equally common *wandering snail*, and the tight curl of the *ramshorn* possessing a kind of simple elegance, the like of which is so often discovered in the most unexpected corners of nature's design. Among the cool foliage of the damp river valley, the little *amber snail* is a common terrestrial mollusc of wetland inclination. Also amid the adjacent vegetation there are spiders that exploit the wealth of invertebrate life. The long-legged *Tetragnetha extensa* is typical of damp habitats, slinging their webs among the fringing pond-side plants, guaranteed success given the huge numbers of tiny flies, midges and mosquitoes that are drawn to the still waters to lay their eggs.

And in the crustaceans we find a vital component of the freshwater food chain. Commonly referred to as water fleas, the multitudes of tiny *cyclops* and *daphnia* team in the water. Although scarcely more than a millimetre long, in their hundreds and thousands they provide the crucial link for so many other creatures. While they feed on the microscopic organic particles filtered from the water, they are in turn widely predated upon themselves. *Freshwater shrimps* and *waterlouse* ensure a rather less diminutive presence, the latter bearing a great resemblance to their land-dwelling counterparts.

The insects, though, provide the greatest diversity. Not least among the requirements essential for their aquatic lifestyle is the means to feed and breathe within the confines of their chosen habitat. There are of course those that can extract the oxygen they need from the water, but ironically a great many of the insects that are more easily observed have not dispensed with the need for air, such as the various and often very familiar species of water bugs and beetles.

The *pond skater* is a very common bug, and although not existing beneath the surface, other than as a jelly-covered egg, is ingeniously adapted to its essentially aquatic environment. An opportunistic feeder on dead or dying insects, its motion across the surface film is greatly facilitated by tiny hairs on the feet that trap a layer of air to aid buoyancy. These creatures are not exclusive to this niche, however, as another bug, the *water measurer* – much more slender of build – stalks rather than dashes, probing for prey immediately below the surface.

Beneath the surface the bugs become increasingly bizarre in appearance. *Water boatman*, alongside the *pond skater*, are among the most recognisable of all aquatic invertebrates. Oar-like hind legs lend them their name and propel the insects jerkily through the water, leaving the other two pairs free to grasp their unfortunate prey; unfortunate because on capture, the *boatman* will pierce its body with the beak-like rostrum that comprise its mouthparts. Digestive enzymes are injected, the resulting juices sucked out – a gruesome exchange.

There are many different species of *water boatman*. The *backswimmer* is readily recognisable, given their habit of swimming upside down and displaying their light, silvery underside. The various species of so-called *lesser water boatman* are smaller and less inclined to visit the surface.

Water stick insects and *water scorpions* are no less distinctive in their appearance, each named for their similarities to the entirely unrelated creatures that they resemble. Both species have in common the long breathing tubes located on the tip of the abdomen to gain air from above the surface. They employ the characteristic feeding method of extracting the juices from their prey through specially developed mouthparts, the *water scorpion* using its pincer-like forelimbs to ensure a firm grip. Although frequent inhabitants of Essex ponds, these insects are rarely seen from land, the *scorpion* enjoying the murk of muddy, sometimes stagnant ponds, the *stick insect* favouring those waters with an abundance of aquatic vegetation.

Aquatic beetles will throw up less physiological surprises, but still deploy no less fascinating adaptations to life in the water. In some, the problem of air supply is solved by means of holding air between body and the elytra (the hardened wing cases), explaining the common sight of small black beetles ascending from the depths, briefly dabbing the surface as if some kind of dare, before darting away back down. Air is taken in via spiracles, gaseous exchange organs situated on the abdomen. Other beetles do not need to make regular visits to the surface. Some species are covered in minutely fine hairs that trap a layer of air around them. As the beetle respires through its spiracles, oxygen is taken in from the surrounding water to replace that consumed by it. In effect, this film of air acts much the same as a gill.

In spite of their less outlandish appearance, compared with some of the water bugs, water beetles nevertheless exhibit a great deal of variety. In Essex ponds the impressive *great diving beetle* will often be present. At several centimetres long, it is one the larger species and voracious predators of invertebrates and even small amphibians and fish. Small, black beetles zipping among the weed are very likely to be *Ilybius* beetles, the very similar species of which can be hard to distinguish from each other. Perhaps the most familiar though, are the *whirligig beetles* that whirl and spin on the surface of still and slow-moving waters, often in great number.

Unlike the bugs, beetles experience a complete metamorphosis, the larva requiring a period of pupation before taking the very different appearance of the adults. Immature bugs will generally look like miniature versions of the mature insects. But what these larvae do have in common with their parents is their predatory behaviour. However, of all the carnivorous larva that hunt the myriad freshwater creatures, there is one group of insects that rather steal the show. Dragonflies and damselflies (collectively known as *Odonata*) live the majority of their lives in the water, and their nymphs are as efficient predators as the nimble winged adults.

Just as the colourful, flying adults inspire awe within the onlooker, the nymphs, when closely examined, exhibit much of the same perfection in their adaptation to their domain, albeit rather less obviously. Most remarkable is the weaponry with which they capture their prey. Whether secreted among the vegetation or obscured by the mud of the pond or river floor, they rely on ambush and uniquely modified mouthparts. The lower lip, or labium, is present as a double-hinged appendage, armed at the tip by deadly spines used to impale the hapless prey – often invertebrates and, with larger species, tadpoles or small fish. As soon as their patient vigil is rewarded by a passing meal – unaware of the impending danger – the labium is unfolded and unleashed with such speed that an unsuccessful attack can be followed up again with repeated strikes. Dragonfly larvae will shed their skin several times in order to accommodate their growth. The final moult takes place out of the water, clinging to an emergent stem or leaf when the time is right for the adult to emerge. The shed skin, or exuvia, that remains after the insect has flown shows the appearance of the nymph in perfect detail, right down to the venation of the wings and the extraordinary labium.

Out of the water, the *Odonata* are arguably without equal for the colour and excitement they bring to a wetland scene subdued by the summer heat. The diminutive damselflies, without the power and presence of their larger cousins, sparkle against the lush green of the adjacent vegetation, whether the scarlet of *large red damselflies* or the vivid blue of the *azure*. The dragonflies are the epitome of successful evolution, essentially unaltered for 250 million years. Eyes are alert to the slightest movement, shimmering wings capable of skilful twists and dashing dives in pursuit of insect prey that may amazingly even include smaller dragonflies, creatures that possess the same aerobatic proficiency as themselves.

Essex has more than twenty species of *Odonata*. They are inspirational creatures that can enthral the obsessive and layman alike. Of the dragonflies, the *emperor dragonfly* is the largest, with wings ten centimetres across, supported on a bright green thorax, the abdomen strikingly blue. Not much smaller are the *brown* and *southern hawkers*, both common in the county.

There are the chasers – the *scarce chaser*, an uncommon and local resident of the quiet river stretches of the north, the *broad-bodied chaser*, with a liking for muddy ponds, and the *black-tailed skimmer*, a frequent colonist of new lakes and gravel pits. The males of all three are beautifully coloured with a dusting of pale, pastel blue. The *darters* are small dragonflies typified by the deep red of the males of the *common* and *ruddy* species, the females with yellow-brown coloration. And on favoured ponds within Epping Forest the *Downy Emerald* speeds low across the water, its bronzed green visage very much one of a woodland setting. They are nationally of limited distribution and very much a jewel in Epping's splendidly embellished *Odonata* crown.

The damselfly is a more delicate beauty, light of build and bright of colour. Some will nonetheless dwarf the smaller species of dragonfly. The *demoiselles* are the most robust of the damselflies and are insects of moving water. Two species occur in Essex. The *banded demoiselle* is thankfully widely distributed in the county, accepting even the habitats that at first hand seem too narrow or overgrown – thankfully, because this is one of the most beautiful of all *Odonata*. They bob through the air with a graceful butterfly-like flight that can easily fool the observer on the initial moments of a first meeting, the metallic blue iridescence of the males ignited in the sun. Along with emerald green females, their presence as they gather, sparkling among the riverside vegetation, is a true joy. The *beautiful demoiselle* is very scarce in Essex and worthy of much of the same celebration of its more widespread relative. The more complete pigmentation of the wings is easily recognisable from the eponymous banding of the other.

Other damselflies generally conform to the more popular image of brightly coloured and slightly built insects. The *large red damselfly* signifies the beginning of the *Odonata* year. While many long for the first swallow, some may just as eagerly scour the pond edge for the first sighting of this spring usher of a different kind, perhaps appearing during the final throes of April, but more usually the early days of May. The dazzling cerulean flash of the *azure damselfly* soon follows. Between them, the *reds* and *azures* may occur in glorious abundance, skimming low over the weedy waters, hovering and threading their way among the pond-side plants in their dozens. The *common blue* provides an identification challenge to distinguish them from the *azure*. One feature is the 'ace of spades' marking on the second segment of the abdomen, different from the 'U'-shaped marking of the *azure*. Then add to the spectrum the gleaming green of the *emerald damselflies*: two species that includes, of course, the rare *scarce emerald*, an insect of coastal grazing marshes.

While the damselflies and dragonflies may be the first to attract our attention, there are other insects that emerge from the depths, having spent their formative time in a similarly aquatic larval state. Given the popular notion that they only live for a day, few sights can seem more desperate than the *mayfly* as it hauls its way out of the water, dragging itself almost forlornly into the air; so urgent is its need to fulfil its short adult life. Above the flowing waters of Essex rivers, *Ephemera* mayflies dance their fateful ballet. The reality is that the insect, although indeed doomed to a brief time on the wing (a matter of hours to a few days, dependent on species), has lived the great majority of its life underwater, grazing on algae and other plant matter. They lack the initial wow of the dragonflies, but close examination reveals a beauty of their own; pearly wings, clear but for a single dark smudge, held gracefully above the body, their abdomen tipped with three long, streaming tails. A number of species occur and the still waters of pond and lake will have their own representatives.

Along with would-be dragons and short-lived ballet dancers, clean freshwater supports many other insects. *Alderflies* may be common. Charcoal-shaded, boldly veined wings are used rather reluctantly during daylight hours, preferring to crawl about among the plants and objects of the water's edge. Their larvae are another of the numerous carnivorous invertebrates. With moth-like flight *caddis flies* buzz from bank to bank, smoky brown wings capturing the mood of the lazy hum of summer-time, although only some species are active by day. In the water the omnivorous nymphs display the kind of inventive adaptation we might come to expect of aquatic life. The majority of *caddis* larvae protect their soft, vulnerable bodies by constructing larval cases, fashioned using frag-ments of plant material, small stones or sand grains, attached to a silken tube spun around the body. Only the head and legs will protrude from the neatly built case, providing superb camouflage. Is that just a twig or other piece of debris or does something dwell inside?

Some creatures winging their way above the surface that have the ini-tial appearance of moths will in fact turn out to be moths. Remarkably, some species have evolved aquatic larvae. *China-mark* moths feed on aquatic plants. The *small china-mark*, a little white moth that is easily put up from waterside vegetation, uses the floating *duckweed* as its foodplant. The caterpillars hibernate and feed in a case made up of the foodplant and pupate below the surface in a silken cocoon. Aquatic caterpillars – whatever next?

Freshwater Vertebrates: Profiting from the Plenty

Whether on the open waters of gravel pit and reservoir, muddy wet marsh or sleepy river backwaters, larger creatures will always be present to take advantage of the burgeoning richness of life held within. Finding them provides us with challenges of varying difficulty. In due season the reservoir does little to conceal its ornithological treasures, sifting out the individual species from the massed flotilla of winter visitors offering up an alternative problem. By contrast, aquatic mammals are predictably elu-sive and the freshwater fish and amphibians are often seen as fleetingly as the invertebrate oddities with which they share their habitats.

Nevertheless, with patience there will always be opportunity. The cleaner stretches of Essex rivers can be full of fish. Where they run clear their piscine residents can be more easily observed. Barbel-mouthed *gud-geon* stay close to the ground, blending in well with riverbed, but get the eye in and they may be found to occur in some number. *Roach* shoal out in the mid-stream. Small members of the carp family, exceptionally attaining a length of forty centimetres, these are attractive little fish, their silvery scales flashing as the sunlight catches their twists and turns. *Chub* can be numerous in places. Red fins perhaps at first cause confusion with *roach* or *rudd*, but are darker in colour and of a more narrow, almost cigar-shaped profile, and big too, maybe as long as eighty centimetres.

Perch may be seen close to the bank as they pass across the gaps in the marginal vegetation. They are a rather handsome fish, with their olive green, striped body, decorated with red pelvic and anal fins on the under-side, one of the pair of dorsal fins brandishing strong spines capable of spiking an unwary angler carelessly removing the fish from its hook. Like most fish, they consume a variety of freshwater invertebrates, but larger individuals will feed exclusively on other fish.

But as much of a predator of other vertebrates as the *perch* are, there is no fiercer freshwater marauder than the *pike*, not only of other fish but also young birds, mammals and amphibians. Everything about them is designed with hunting in mind. Cryptic markings allow them to blend seamlessly with the submerged vegetation. From motionless concealment within their weedy recess, a rapid attack enables them to ambush unwary prey before their peril becomes apparent, powerful jaws equipped with sharp teeth administering a deadly grip. In an instant the restful river erupts into a momentary flurry of deadly activity as the peaceful shoals scatter in panic.

Although dwelling in the relative concealment of the water, the most frequently encountered river vertebrates will tend to be the fish, as mammals here are few and extremely secretive. As with anywhere else, their sightings provide an added thrill to the occasion.

The aquatic mammal fauna of Essex has seen eventful times over the recent decades, few more so than the *water vole*. They have suffered through pollution, habitat fragmentation and isolation and even the intro-duction of the *American mink*, although county records of this alien pred-ator have been few, pointing the finger of blame more squarely at the other forms of human interference.

Thankfully, in spite of their decline, *water voles* are still present along all Essex river systems, as well as certain marshland localities. If we are lucky, that loud plop as we approach the river bank might be followed by a view of a stocky, blunt-nosed rodent paddling its way across the water, disap-pearing among the edging plants where its burrow entrance might be hid-den. Within their subterranean retreat the highly reproductive *water vole* might rear as many as five litters of the same number of young, neces-sary mathematics given an average life expectancy of just five and a half months. As far as its diet is concerned, they are onto a sure winner, requiring nothing more than the succulent parts of riverside grasses, rushes and sedges. An exceptionally quiet approach could just be rewarded by the endearing image of the vole hunched on the bank, intently munching its way through some green delicacy.

Few people will ever be so privileged as to see an *otter* wild in an Essex river, but so exciting is the return of this wonderful creature to the county that no writing on Essex wetlands could be complete without their mention. Anyone so fortunate as to see one would have been privy to an unforgettable wildlife experience. They move both about the land and through water with adeptness, although it is in the latter that they come into their own. A sleek, streamlined body glides effortlessly through the water, even in the dark those long whiskers can feel their way around in pursuit of their aquatic prey.

Their decline was startling and absolute. By the 1970s, habitat loss and pollution from the organochlorine fertilisers – that had similarly almost accounted for the *sparrowhawk* population – had taken its heavy toll. A program of reintroduction in the East Anglian region, started in the 1980s, included their reappearance in suitable stretches of Essex rivers. Their slow increase since shows promise. The successful recovery of the otter population in the county would surely represent one the greatest triumphs of conservation in Essex.

With the abundant insect life associated with freshwater, such habitats are of great importance to bats. They are associated with other habitats. Many roost in buildings and old trees, foraging around woods, along hedgerows and provide a dash of night-time enigma to our urban parks and gardens. Freshwater, however, is a habitat of primary significance to bats. One in particular is especially suited to hunting over water. *Daubenton's bats* skim low over the surface, shallow wing-beats allow them to fly low enough to capture emerging *mayflies, caddis flies* and even pluck aquatic insects from the surface of the water. Many that twist and dive over the river or lake surface would have travelled far to forage there. *Pipistrelles*, for example, roost in buildings and will journey several kilometres if the pickings are rich. During dusk before the light fades completely, they can hypnotise with their impossible twists and daring dives in pursuit of the innumerable small insects that buzz invisibly above the surface; insects invisible to us but not to the remarkable faculty of echolocation.

Other insectivores frequent the waterways. Away from the rivers, *water shrews* prefer to inhabit quick flowing streams, although on occasion they are not averse to some still-water habitats, such as ponds or gravel pits. They will forage on land but are chiefly predators of aquatic crustaceans and insect larvae. Long sensitive whiskers enable them to seek out prey when submerged, water-repellent fur facilitating easier movement through the water. As with other small, largely nocturnal mammals, their elusiveness somewhat belies the extent of the Essex population. Although certainly not as numerous as the abundant *common shrew* and tied closely to aquatic habitats, they are probably fairly widespread across the county. That rustle in the streamside undergrowth might just be the sound of something a little bit different.

Given the so very effective secrecy of aquatic mammals, it is with the amphibians that we are far more likely to be familiar, especially as they have been increasingly attracted to our back yards via the garden pond. Even without this pleasing modern trend, many a childhood acquaintance with our amphibious neighbours would have been made, entertaining us long before the advent of the computer generation. Easter holidays would have been spent capturing newts from the local amphibian hotspots. We might look back on ourselves with scorn for our arguably dubious behaviour, as we remember the thrill of catching that prized *great-crested newt* that are, of course, now protected by law. But how many imaginations did this capture? How often has the excitement of discovery created the spark that grew through the formative years into a deeply passionate appreciation of the wonders of nature in adult life? With such first-hand experience of our local environment and the gamut of wildlife within, many a seed has been sown.

All three British newts are to be found in Essex. *Smooth newts* are the most common and widespread. A male in breeding condition is a rather splendid little beast, with his fine crest and orange-spotted belly. Outside the breeding season they are more similar in appearance to the *palmate newt*, especially the females. The breeding male *palmate* will sport the significantly webbed feet from which they gain their name, a smooth crest and the thread-like tip to the tail. *Palmates*, although common over much of Britain, are rather scarce animals in Essex. In the acidic moorland pools of upland Britain they essentially replace the *smooth newt*. Where they are common in Essex, it is often in those water bodies with similar pH tendencies; the pond in Pound Wood probably holds as many *palmate* as it does *smooth newts*.

There is little about the *great-crested* that can be confused with their cousins. They have suffered much decline and are now afforded legal protection. At around sixteen centimetres in length and more stoutly built, they dwarf the others. They are also much the rarest and most elusive of the three, preferring larger ponds and spending the most time in water; most *smooth* and *palmate newts* have left their breeding pools by early summer, leaving the feathery gilled tadpoles as proof of their earlier residency. The *great crested newt* is quite an impressive creature. Its dark brown, black-spotted body, adorned in the males with a jagged crest, looks almost black in the water, a flash of the fiery orange belly offering a striking contrast.

Of all the amphibians, the *common frog* and *toad* require the least introduction. For many they represent as much a part of the back garden scene as the intent supervision of the *robin* when we dig over the soil. The unexpected hop among the herbaceous border of the smooth-skinned *frog* can still deliver a start, no matter how many times it happens, the more measured crawl of the warty *toad* more likely be spotted out of the corner of the eye rather than causing surprise as it endeavours to creep unnoticed from cover to cover. In our ponds we can delight at the transformation from the tiny comma of the tadpole as it struggles from its egg, growing and sprouting its little legs, eventually assuming the impossibly miniature form of their parents.

It is in the garden where we are most likely to hear the quiet, nocturnal croaking of the male frogs as they emerge during late winter to find mates. In the wider countryside these clandestine gatherings are rather rarely encountered, the resulting mass of spawn hidden among the weedy shallows of the pond edge. Indeed, the tiny St Peter's Marsh nature reserve in Braintree was established principally for its importance as a frog breeding site. The toads deposit theirs as gelatinous strands, curled around the erect stems of water plants.

While the frog is a much more terrestrial creature than many give it credit for, the toad is even more so, and as such may be more likely to be seen crawling about the undergrowth quite unexpectedly where there may be an apparent lack of aquatic habitat. As long as there is damp daytime retreat and somewhere for a dip if things heat up too much, the *common toad* will be free to roam the undergrowth for the slugs and insects that comprise their diet.

In the water, full-grown amphibians find relative safety, save for the keen eye and stabbing bill of the *heron*. But even here lurks a waterborne threat from what some might regard as an unlikely quarter. There are many misnomers in nature, one such being the *grass snake*. Although spending some time hunting on land, where they may haunt the water margins and damp meadows, this is a creature entirely at home in the water where it is a voracious predator of aquatic vertebrates, mainly amphibians. With ease they wind their way across the surface, their green scaled body more than a metre in length, maybe even two, forming an effortless sinuous 'S', creating only a slight ripple as it goes, its yellow-collared head held just above the surface. Where our eyes may be tuned to spotting the flick of a newt as it leaves the cover of submerged plants, ascending for a gulp of air, or the superbly camouflaged head of the frog peeping above the surface, the sleekness of the *grass snake* sliding over the water adds that extra dash of intrigue to an already mysterious aquatic haven.

The inland freshwaters of Essex can deliver ornithological spectacles to rival those of the coast, with the passage birdwatching and winter congregations of the Hanningfield and, in particular, Abberton Reservoirs rivalling that to be had anywhere else in the county. Late summer brings the autumn wader passage, when *ruff* and *common sandpiper* are among the most frequent at either locality. But in times of low water level and a more extensive shoreline of exposed mud, the list of potential visitors is impressive. More easy to find are the *spotted redshank*, a taller, more elegant version of its very widespread relative, and the *black-tailed godwits*. In good years at Abberton, armed with a telescope and lots of patience, you might just be able to pick out the miniscule *little stint*, a wader even smaller than the *dunlin, curlew sandpiper* and exceptionally, *wood sandpiper*.

The invasion of winter wildfowl is as impressive a sight as any. For those with a more general appreciation, the skeins of geese as they sweep in across the water overhead gives a thrilling sight in itself before we even begin to sort out the *Canada* from the *greylag* from the *white-fronts*. So too do the massed rafts of ducks that fill the gently swelling water. For those with a keenness for birding there are the *goldeneye* and *goosander* to pick out, or even such scarcities as *smew*: either the chestnut-capped female or the delicately pied male. And there is the further excitement of the rarer species of *grebe* with possibility of *red-necked, slavonian* and *black-necked*.

Come the spring, and like their coastal counterparts, the reservoirs become much quieter places. Interest is maintained by *common terns* that nest on special rafts and the *yellow wagtails* that scurry along the moss covered banks, alongside the resident *pied*. Only the flocks of *swift, swallows* and *martins* attracted to the emergence of waterborne flies recalls the plenty of winter. Many of the waterbirds that stay to breed, like *little grebe, gadwall* and *coot*, are those that also find sanctuary in the more secluded environs of recolonised gravel pits.

With the splendour of the *great crested grebe* we are left to while away the spring and summer with one of our most beautiful birds. A bird of slender build, adorned with plush head feathers, fanned out to full effect when engaged in their head to head courtship display. So different are the stripy-headed young that when small enough will ride in the warmth and safety of a parent's back, barely visible but for that little pied head peeping our from among the feathers.

While the appearance of gravel pits has enhanced the breeding possibilities for a number of wetland birds, they cannot provide the same opportunities for those of the freshwater marsh. From the loss of this habitat followed the reduction of Essex breeding populations of such birds as *redshank* and *lapwing* that require the wet, tussocky grassland in which to nest. It is along the fine stretch of the Ingrebourne Marshes, which lie partially within the boundaries of Hornchurch Country Park, that these birds, among others, can raise their young. Various other habitats are associated with that of the marsh or fen. Surreptitious birds may haunt the tall vegetation, like *sedge* and even *grasshopper warblers*, from the tops of occasional sallow *reed buntings* might chirp the claim to its patch of marsh, while areas of *reed* will attract *reed warblers* and perhaps even the champion of all skulkers, the *water rail*.

Along the river, too, many small birds might be seen, flitting among the vegetation or darting from bank to bank, but one in particular always provides that extra bit of magic to that sleepy backwater scene. It is of course, the *kingfisher*, so often described as a jewel of the riverbank, and rightly so. This is the classic bird of quite waterways, not only of rivers and canals, but also secluded lakes. Even the most fleeting sight of its electric blur as it speeds past is always keenly sought after and so richly enjoyed. Even where present they can frustrate with their reluctance to be seen. Territorial birds along their stretch of river, patience and a touch of 'right place at the right time' is required if we are to see that bolt of colour flash past. A suitable territory must have some sheltering trees and vertical banks in which to excavate a metre-long tunnel and nest chamber, using their bill at first and later their feet. Only the very fortunate will be able to observe the bird as it hunts for small fish. Motionless, they will wait on a favoured perch, watching beneath the ripples for any telltale movement. In spite of their bright colouring, the contrasting blue and orange hues serve to break up their outline against the background, making them surprisingly hard to see. A moment of quick-fire accuracy and it is plunging into the water, before flapping its way clear with a beak full of fish – a rare but wonderful image of the simple beauty and drama of nature.

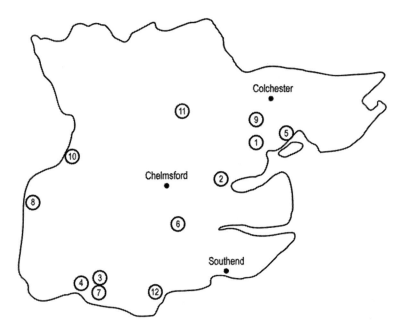

WETLAND HABITATS IN ESSEX

1. Abberton Reservoir

(Explorer 184, Grid Reference 963 185)

A vast 480ha area of open water and an excellent site for birdwatching. Many thousands of wildfowl spend the winter and an interesting stream of waders occur on passage, both including frequent rarities. Scrub surrounding Essex Wildlife Trust Visitor Centre adds interest.

2. Chigborough Lakes

(Exp 183, GR 877 086)

A series of old gravel pits now well colonised by wildlife. Lakes attract wintering waterfowl and breeding species. Adjacent willows and scrub are alive with small birds and more open, grassy areas hold interesting plants, such as *common spotted* and *southern marsh orchids*.

3. Cranham Marsh

(Exp 175, GR 567 856)

A small but interesting remnant of marshland habitat – an island in a sea of agriculture and suburbia. Fen vegetation includes such typical plants as *meadowsweet* and *hemp-agrimony*. Wooded areas enhance the interest of the site, with woodland birds and flora living alongside the rich vegetation and insect life of the open grassland and marsh.

4. DAGENHAM CHASE
(Exp 175, GR 515 855)

Within the depths of metropolitan Essex this important London Wildlife Trust reserve is comprised of nearly 50ha of wetland, grassland and scrub habitat. Old gravel pits attract many birds on passage and in winter, including *snipe, lapwing, shoveler, teal* and *wigeon*.

5. FINGRINGHOE WICK
(Exp 184, GR 041 195)

Part of the exceptional wildlife value of this nature reserve, shaped and contoured by gravel extraction decades past, lies within a number of ponds and a large lakes. A varied aquatic flora includes *water-plantain*, dragonflies and damselflies, and a number of wetland birds breed, including *little grebe* and *kingfisher*.

6. HANNINGFIELD RESERVOIR
(Exp 175, GR 725 972)

Perhaps rather overshadowed by Abberton, the smaller (a mere 360ha) reservoir at Hanningfield is still an exceptional location for the birdwatcher. Winter numbers are impressive and scarce birds always turn up, such as the rarer species of *grebe*. Adjacent woodland adds a great deal to the Hanningfield experience. From the Essex Wildlife Trust visitor centre nature trails lead through mixed broadleaved and coniferous woodland full with its associated wildlife.

7. INGREBOURNE MARSHES
An important swathe of freshwater marsh along the River Ingrebourne, part of which resides in the Hornchurch Country Park (Exp 175, GR 535848). It is an important habitat for breeding birds, like *redshank* and *lapwing*, as well as a huge variety of wetland plants. Grassland, scrub and young woodland of the country park adds further interest.

8. RIVER LEA REGIONAL PARK
(Exp 174, GR 377 033)

A huge area of old gravel workings along the banks of the River Lea and River Lee Navigation. The complex of open water, river and dykes unsurprisingly attract many birds (eg Hall Marsh Exp 174, GR 372 018 and Holyfield Lake Exp 174, GR 374 045) An outstanding area for *Odonata*, especially at the Dragonfly Sanctuary along Cornmill Stream (Exp 174, GR 378 017).

9. ROMAN RIVER VALLEY
(Exp 184, GR 975 211)

A marvellous fragment of river valley habitat occupies part of this reserve alongside adjacent woodland. This is one of very few Essex locations for the *beautiful demoiselle*, occurring here alongside the widespread *banded demoiselle*. Many other invertebrates are to be found, such as *mayflies*, *alderfly* and *amber snails*.

10. SAWBRIDGEWORTH MARSH
(Exp 194, GR 493 158)

A splendid little marshland nature reserve beside the River Stort, encompassing areas of marsh, damp meadow and willow woodland. A rich flora includes *marsh arrowgrass*, *southern marsh orchid* and *marsh willowherb*, and many invertebrates occur, including *red-eyed damselfly* along the river.

11. ST PETER'S MARSH
(Exp 195, GR 757 237)

Only a fifth of a hectare in area, this spring-fed marsh is important as a traditional site for breeding frogs.

12. STANFORD WARREN
(Exp 175, GR 687 812)

This 10ha reserve is comprised largely of an extensive reed-bed, filling the site of 1920s gravel extraction. In spring the reeds ring to the churring of *reed warblers,* accompanied by the plaintive call of the *cuckoo* who target the warbler's nests for their parasitic egg-laying behaviour. *Water rail* have bred and *bearded tits* visit in winter.

CHAPTER SIX

Nature the Opportunist

Think of the wilder parts of Essex and it might be the sultry summertime grasslands and their leafy woodland neighbours, or the ever-shifting coastline towards which the inland rivers trace their inexorable course that we will be drawn towards. Such places have, of course, experienced much change at the hand of the altering influence of human doings. But as these more significant components of wild Essex have been modified, other niches have arisen, born of much more recent origins.

Often such new opportunities are easily appreciated, such as the gravel pit lakes (easily applicable here but explored in the previous chapter) that give rise to habitats that will always elicit a perception of naturalness, in spite of their industrial connections. In other instances though, the wildlife in their midst may provide something more of a surprise. In many instances we might hesitate to consider them as part of the mainstay of wildlife habitat in the county. It would be easy to view them as mere bit-part players, easy and probably quite correct, but by way of epilogue their mention should be made. Often they will provide green spaces in circumstances where such environs are sorely needed; at times they ensure an unlikely recess for wild plants and animals where their options are limited.

Like the worked out gravel pits, some of these 'modern' habitats give a sense of agedness, irrespective of their comparative youth. Plantation forestry is scattered across Essex, mainly in the northern half of the county, without there being the large forests that have been planted in other parts of East Anglia. In spite of the rather obvious artificiality of rows of *sitka spruce* and the like, they can nevertheless, achieve a feeling of grandness, with the rusty trunks spearing ram-rod straight towards the sky and the jagged horizon provided by their evergreen 'Christmas Tree' foliage. Their wildlife value is of course limited when compared to their native deciduous counterparts, but such residents as the *goldcrest* and *coal tit* find favourable habitat among the cones and the needles.

The appearance of new woodland has not rested solely with the advent of commercial forestry. At the turn of the 20th century the first stages of an unlikely source of future woodland took place. As the 19th century became the 20th, the Plotlands came about, as areas of agricultural land in south Essex were put to auction as small holdings. They were made available to locals but particular efforts were made to target the people of East London, who it was thought could be encouraged to escape the city for the rural idyll. As the plots were bought up, communities began to develop and estates of simple and sometimes very basic housing grew. Many were purchased as weekend retreats, away from the bustle and grime of the city, but a number were bought with permanent residency in mind. However, these settlements tended to possess poor facilities, where a lack of mains water and adequate sewage systems often proved problematic. In the decades following the Second World War most of the plotland dwellings had been abandoned and demolished in favour of more organised development, while new planning regulations prevented the growth of any new plotland communities in the future.

But what of their connection with the wildlife of Essex? Some areas of the old plotlands, although long deserted, escaped this new phase of development and in the decades that passed once more succumbed to the pervasive touch of nature.

As with anywhere else, the process of vegetative succession, if uninterrupted, will win out in the end. Secondary woodland develops, characterised by a community of *oak* and *hawthorn*. They will lack the floral richness of ancient woodlands but certainly cannot be described as poor wildlife habitats. Many plants occur and flourish, like such common but colourful plants as *herb robert* and *wood avens*.

Alongside the native colonisers, orchard trees and garden flowers might persist to keep the botanists on their toes. Of those that we find today, the Dunton Hill component of the Langdon Nature Reserve, a survivor of the Basildon New Town development, is the most expansive remnant, complete with an intact plotland home, 'The Haven', now a museum. The hectares of scrub that have spread among the old road system always contain the flitter of songbirds – the *redwing* and *fieldfare* of winter, gorging on the abundant haws, or the springtime warble of *blackcap* and *whitethroat*.

Smaller pockets can be found elsewhere. Conservation management has converted one in particular, the Rochford District Council-owned Grove Wood, from a thorny tangle into an attractive, accessible woodland, where *purple hairstreaks* flutter about the oak crowns as they do in their more aged habitats and the spring song of the *chiff chaff* echoes among the trees with similar resonance.

It is the onward march of colonisation that draws these places back into the natural realm, healing the scars of our past activities and blurring the boundaries between human inhabitation and the domain of the wild plants and creatures. Not always will this represent a trade off, where the habitats that arise after the act tend not be as rich as those previously lost.

Set in the thick of the urban Thamesside sprawl is the Grays Chalk Quarry nature reserve. Descend the steps down onto the old quarry floor and one could scarcely move into a realm more in contrast to the homogenous housing and bustling townscape beyond.

This hole in the ground, that comprises the greater part of this sixteen-hectare reserve, has become largely reclaimed by new woodland, whose canopy offers a welcoming shield to the urbanity above. But the real treasure is the marvellous assemblage of calcareous plants whose need for chalky soil renders them great local scarcities. The clay soils that prevail over the greater part of the county effectively fill a bowl of chalk, composed of the bodies of prehistoric marine life and set down some fifty million years ago when what we now know as Essex comprised an ocean floor.

Where the chalk comes to the surface in the most southerly reaches a flora occurs that is most untypical of the greater area. *Horseshoe vetch* and the blue composite flower of *chicory* may have been encountered on the ridge path on the way to the reserve, but the quarry bottom holds further delights. Besides other scarce plants, like *deadly nightshade* and *round-leaved wintergreen*, *orchids* grow here. Some such as *twayblade* are numerous and other less common species might be revealed to those who make a closer search. And with the chalk-loving plants that thrive, so too do unusual insects; *grayling* butterfly and the *chalk carpet* moth are of very limited distribution in the county. Not only can we easily forget that we are in the middle of town, but also that we are in Essex altogether, surrounded as we may be by plant and invertebrate life more expected of the North Downs across the Thames in Kent.

As we look around for the less obvious opportunities where wildlife can prosper, or at least maintain a toehold, we may find that they come from some unlikely sources. Several stretches of former railway line have now become places for nature. Even where the trains still rumble through their value as wildlife areas is unseen – obviously due to their inaccessibility – and underestimated. Save for the thunder of passing rolling stock the scrub-covered embankments and cuttings are scarcely troubled by trampling feet and in this respect are relatively undisturbed. Thus, these narrow corridors have the potential to allow the plants and animals of the countryside to infiltrate deeper into the towns than would otherwise be likely. Pioneering plants like *willowherbs* and *ox-tongue* may be quick to colonise any areas of ground left bare.

For those who work on the trackside, the rustle and scurry of lizards is commonplace, enjoying the heat of the sun-drenched banks, and it is hard to imagine another way that *badgers* could live so close to the centre of Southend as they do, were it not for safety and concealment afforded by these well-vegetated strips of urban habitat.

Where the rail network was rightly or wrongly deemed superfluous to the needs of the Essex public, parts of their former course were soon reclaimed. In addition to the twenty-four kilometre length of the Flitch Way County Park, running between Bishop's Stortford and Braintree, three sections now rank among the nature reserves of the Essex Wildlife Trust. In the north, the Colne Valley Railway reserve commands fine views across the river valley of the same name and beyond, whilst protecting a couple of hectares of habitat for nesting birds and woodland flowers. Further south, the other two reserves encompass stretches of the old Maldon to Woodham Ferrers line. The two-and-a-half kilometre stretch of Maldon Wick has come to contain a rich assemblage of plants and insects. Numerous wildflowers grow below a tree canopy that includes *wild service*, and a wealth of invertebrates is made obvious by the many butterflies that flit between the sunny clearings created among the shade.

Of the twenty-eight butterfly species recorded at Maldon Wick, the *white-letter hairstreak* is one of the more notable, an insect that the Wick has in common with Stow Maries Halt. Just a few hundred metres of the old line runs within this small nature reserve, but along with an adjoining area of land this is a splendid little oasis for wildlife. Even before leaving the road to enter the thorny woodland that has developed along the cutting, the sides of the old bridge catch our attention, dotted as it is with fronds of small ferns: *maidenhair spleenwort*, *wall rue* and *black spleenwort* are all scarce plants in this fern impoverished county.

Along the floor of the cutting the sound of the plentiful birds obscured within can frustrate with their shyness to be seen, but ultimately deliver warmth and cheer – perhaps the plaintive toot of the *bullfinch*, before tantalising us with a flash of the white rump and a glimpse of that deep pink, barrel chest as it disappears into cover, or maybe the wonderful, descending tones of the *willow warbler*, trickling down from its perch atop one the oaks that has grown up among the *blackthorn* scrub.

Adjacent to the former railway line an area of grassland abuts, perhaps an unlikely spot to find troops of *common spotted orchids* and the inconspicuous presence of another of the reserve's fern species, the *adder's-tongue*. Here also a summer swathe of *fleabane* arises, the riot of the yellow blooms too much of a temptation for the likes of the *common blue* to ignore. Mr Beeching's loss is wildlife's gain.

In this land where wildlife has been increasingly ushered away to the peripheries, it is towards the frontier habitats, like the railway lines, that it may have to turn. Even in more ordinary circumstances and in the wider context it is often such boundaries as provided by the riverbank or hedgerow that offer retreat from an intensively used landscape.

And of the more unlikely refuges, the similarly linear green space of the roadside verge is another that can provide such respite. They may be given little thought as we dash by in the car. At forty miles per hour the flowers of *red campion* and *greater stitchwort* are just a blur, the trill of the *chaffinch* heard only as a brief, dulcet snapshot, the full score of its pleasant jingle left to our imagination. The disturbance caused by the ever-increasing traffic and the pollution associated with it is bound to have some effect, but a surprising wealth of flora and fauna can occur. Far from encouraging us to use our cars less, the seemingly endless quest for new roads often seems unnecessary and counteractive, but if nature can find some way to adapt, thus softening the impact, so much the better.

The opportunities for wildlife obviously differ with the hugely varying nature of our roads. Along the fast, busy motorways and 'A' roads, broad strips of grassy embankments, encroached on or planted up with trees and shrubs, often slope away either side of the tarmac. Here as with the railways, few people will tread, leaving any would-be residents undisturbed, provided the noise and fumes have not prevented their arrival in the first instance. Certainly there are small mammals, like the *field voles*, that live hidden among the long grass, but their presence is testified by watchful eye of the hovering *kestrel* – so much an icon of roadside wildlife. It is the large birds that are obviously more easily seen from the windows of a speeding car, if only the *rooks* eying up the inevitable road kill, putting themselves at similar risk as they attempt to snatch a beakful between vehicles.

It may take a traffic jam to appreciate the less conspicuous. At a slower pace the umbellifer-like heads of *yarrow* (in fact a member of the daisy family) and the single yellow flowers of *sowthistle* might be noticed. Not always will the more typically wayside plants be the only ones present. There are *cowslips* that carpet the banks around certain stretches of Basildon roadside; whether planted or naturally occurring it is a spring-time vision that will brighten any journey into work. In places a veritable meadow flora can persist, where *knapweed, ox-eye* and even *wild carrot* bloom among the grasses. They are as irresistible a source of nectar here, as they are in their more typical surroundings, attracting the common grassland butterflies like *small skipper* and *meadow brown*.

The quiet country roads offer different opportunities. The flow of traffic is of course much less, but the buffer zone provided by the roadside verge will tend to be very narrow, not the broader sweep of the motorway embankment. But around the twists and turns along the proverbial country mile, the sights and sounds of the countryside are more easily appreciated. Perhaps accompanied by hedgerows and over-grown ditches, they may serve as wildlife corridors or simply a habitat where plants and animals can find a home. The hedges provide nesting habitat for birds, like *whitethroat, dunnock* or *chaffinch*. From the hedgerow trees a *little owl* may be watchful, surveying the landscape from a favourite perch, scouring the ground for insects that will comprise part of its diet, along with such less unusual owl-prey items as small birds and mammals.

Also on the hunt for the invertebrates that share their grassy domain, the squeak of *common shrews* is often heard from the verge below as they scurry along runs made in the vegetation. They are themselves food for the predatory *weasel* and it is here also that the larger but no less elusive *stoat* might just be seen, bounding along the roadside on the look-out for the rabbits that emerge from the cover of the hedge to nibble on the grass.

Some thought should be given to the wildlife of the farmland. It has certainly known better times, with the uncompromising intensity of modern agriculture so often cited as that which has threatened and mar-ginalised once-common plants and animals. Little or no space is left for formerly numerous agricultural 'weeds', like the *cornflower* and *corncockle*, and sightings of once plentiful birds like the *grey partridge* and *tree sparrow* must be very much sought after. Thankfully though, they do hang on. *Harvest mice* may have time to raise a family before the untimely blades of the combine harvesters raze the cornfields and *hares* still run over the fields in such favoured areas as Canewdon and Wallsea Island beside the River Crouch. The wonderful, sustained song of the *skylark* can be heard floating across on the spring breeze, although at lower density than before, and even though the seasonal feeding provided by over-wintering stubble has declined, the twittering flocks of *buntings* and *finches* can still be seen, looping into the air before disappearing back down to be engulfed by the camouflaging brown fields.

As a response to the desperate plight of the plants and animals asso-ciated with farming, conservation has opened a new front. In 2000 the Essex Wildlife Trust, somewhat fittingly given the turning of the new millennium, purchased a two-hundred-and-eighty-hectare farm on the northern reaches of the Blackwater Estuary. The fields to be planted up as woodland, or sown as new wildflower meadows? No. Breaching of the seawall, in the name of managed retreat, will recreate new areas of graz-ing marsh and saltmarsh, and the nooks that would formerly have allowed wildlife to live alongside the crops, the margins, ditches and copses, will be reinstated, but half the area will still be run as an arable farm. Farming will of course always be a part of countryside, as it has been for time immemorial, but to prove that it need not be unaccommodating to the requirements of nature is as significant a message in the modern world as the protection of important wildlife habitats.

Then there are the component parts of the towns themselves that allow the human residents the pleasure of seeing wildlife on their very own doorstep. Here, in the full face of adversity and surrounded by the harshness of the urban landscape, the wildlife that we find possesses a special fascination, born of its tenacity to endure the relative hardships of town life. There are the gardens, of course, with frog-filled ponds, fruit trees and nectar-yielding flowers, where the *blue tits* in the nest box and speckled juvenile *robins* being fed by their doting parents entertain and delight. There may be wild animals that lurk of a night-time. The *fox* has become a most adept town dweller, taking opportunity from the waste-fulness and, at times, generosity of humans. The lucky ones can be thrilled by the sight of *badgers* in their gardens and how often is the endearing little *hedgehog* ever seen away from inhabitation?

The close-cropped sward of the playing field or park is clearly not going to be a rich habitat, but one that is not entirely bereft of wildlife. *Pied wagtails* and *mistle thrushes* will often be seen pecking around the out-field or centre circle on the cricket or football pitch, sharp eyes alert for tiny insects among the turf, and *starlings* may gather, probing the ground in search of *leatherjackets*. The winter congregation of gulls is another familiar playing field sight, sometimes in flocks two or three hundred strong. Mainly they will be *black-headed*, in their winter garb without the dark hood that gives them their name, but there will almost always be *common gulls* to be sieved out, a few pairs of grey-green legs among a forest of *black-headed* scarlet. The bulk of the *herring* and the dark grey wings of the *lesser black-backed* are much easier to pick out.

Many of the larger town parks are spacious enough to encompass within their bounds quieter situations, removed from the playgrounds and impromptu 'jumpers for goalposts' games of football. Planted *oaks*, *London plane* or magnificent *horse chestnut* may line the paths, formal gardens drone to the tireless toil of bumblebees and ornamental lakes allow close views of waterfowl – the majestic *mute swan* or the cheerfully famil-iar *mallard*, the handsome *Canada goose* or the nervous *coot*.

The parks can indeed be of genuine wildlife value. *Little egrets, spotted flycatchers* and *grey wagtails* have all stopped off at Southend's Priory Park. No doubt regular visitors to urban parks in other parts of the county can include similarly unusual birds on their own species lists.

Sometimes they will truly amaze, dropping the jaw and stopping you in your tracks. There is surely no other recreation ground in Essex, perhaps even further afield, that can boast thousands of *orchids* and a liberal smattering of *yellow rattle*, other than the stunning spectacle at a Basildon park, adjacent to the Essex Wildlife Trust's Langdon Nature Reserve. It is a remarkable sight, bordering on the bizarre. Away down the slope the scene is not an unusual one, children playing on the swings and messing around on the grass, folk walking their dogs. But among a band of sward around the edge of the field, thankfully spared the mower blade, sure enough, in their multitudes are the *green-winged orchids* growing throughout. Does this not prove that it is possible for us to coexist with nature?

When not too neatly kept, the rambling churchyard offers another bolthole for town wildlife. Trees will often be found standing among the headstone – a *holly* perhaps, complete with nesting *blackbirds* grateful for the protection afforded by the spiny foliage, or *yew* trees and their autumn berry bonanza. Such plants as *cow parsley* will ably colonise the unmown edges, their crowded white flower heads bringing a host of insects to the scene. Among these is the *holly blue*, whose spring and autumn foodplants – the tree of the same name and the adventurous *ivy* – are often in plentiful supply.

And the masonry of the graves themselves creates niches for wildlife. *Biting stonecrop* scrambles across and smothers the gravestones, a long way distant from the more maritime situations where it may be more familiar. *Lichens*, potentially many decades old, encrust the headstones. They are easily overlooked but rather amazing organisms, resulting from the symbiosis between an algae and fungus. The more robust fungus offers the algae protection from the elements, while the algae produces food to sustain the fungal component. These are remarkable little plants that in their own understated way do a great deal to remind us just how adaptable and resourceful nature can be in occupying even the most seemingly inhospitable niches.

It is obviously tempting to look upon the woodland and coast, river and heath as we seek to discover the essence of wild Essex. These are the habitats that harbour a great proportion of the richness and diversity of this county's wildlife. The thousands of birds that gather along the winter coastline give Essex international renown. On a national scale, such places as Abberton Reservoir are among the most important ornithological sites in the country and the medieval heritage of Hatfield Forest is of huge historical significance. On a more specific level, there are plants and animals that have their stronghold here or are found nowhere else in the country.

In truth, however, the essence is present wherever we find it. Of all the places that the rare and gorgeous *waxwing* puts in a winter appearance, one of the best localities has in recent years proven to be among the ornamental *rowans* at a supermarket car park in Pitsea. No matter how insalubrious the surroundings may be, a beautiful thing will always be a beautiful thing. It is always thrilling to see rare creatures and plants, to experience that buzz of excitement when finding a beautiful butterfly or stunning orchid for the first time. But is it any less stimulating if our own pond attracts the dashing presence of dragonflies to our very own gardens, regardless of how common they are, allowing us to witness at first hand their remarkable transition from an alien-like aquatic nymph to a glorious winged adult?

Many animals are widespread around the county: their presence as we catch sight of them on our travels might not warrant much of a second glance. *Woodpeckers* are always likely to be encountered on a walk around the fine woodlands of Essex, but when they appear where we least expect them, perhaps during a lunch break at the local park, or swooping over the road on a walk to the shops, then they take on, once again, something of that 'first sighting' quality.

With this in mind, those more unorthodox or more homely situations where nature can be found to prevail, the tall grass at the roadside or the rambling churchyard, although unlikely to engage our imagination in the same way as the wood or meadow, are as essential to the natural tapestry of Essex as anywhere else. They underline the assertion that – even without the great swathes of windswept moorland or the landform of awesome mountain ranges and dramatic gorges hewn in the rock of ages – for those who choose to delve, the possibilities are, for all intents and purposes, endless.

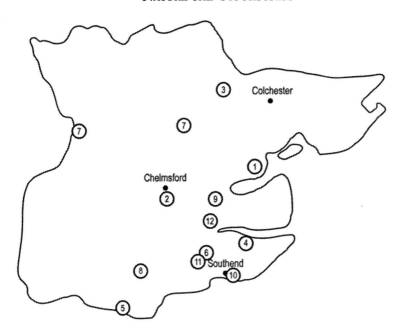

THE OTHER HABITATS OF ESSEX

1. Abbotts Hall Farm
(Explorer 184, Grid Reference 963 146)

An Essex Wildlife Trust farm, where arable production will continue, while encouraging wildlife to return to the farmed landscape. Managed retreat has taken place to allow the creation of new grazing marsh and saltmarsh.

2. Central Park
(Exp 183, GR 703 067)

A town park, close to the centre of Chelmsford, that can deliver a surprising diversity of wildlife. *Great crested grebe* have bred on the lake that can also attract the foraging attentions of bats, such as *pipistrelle* and the large *noctule bat*. *Daubenton's bats* use the River Can that runs through the park, and *water voles* have occasionally been seen. Various dragonflies and damselflies occur, including *brown hawker* and *banded demoiselle*.

3. Colne Valley Railway
(Exp 195, GR 868 292)

A two-hectare strip of former railway line near the River Colne, overlooking the attractive north Essex countryside.

4. RIVER CROUCH (CANEWDON AND WALLASEA ISLAND)
    (Exp 176, GR 923 948)

From the seawall, taken from the Essex Wildlife Trust's Lion Creek reserve, arable fields can be viewed where *brown hares* can still be found and farmland birds like *yellowhammer, corn bunting* and *skylark* can be seen.

5. GRAYS CHALK QUARRY
    (Exp 162, GR 611 787)

An old quarry site, now much wooded and rich in calcareous plants, including *orchids, kidney vetch, deadly nightshade* and *autumn gentian*. A number of interesting invertebrates occur, including such scarce or localised butterflies as *grayling* and *marbled white*.

6. GROVE WOOD
    (Exp 175, GR 825 923)

Conservation management has turned this former plotland into a place full of wildlife. Various wildflowers can be found and butterflies like the *speckled wood* and *purple hairstreak*.

7. FLITCH WAY
    (Exp 195, GR 519 212 - 760 227)

A great variety of wildlife can be found along the twenty-four kilometres of the former Bishop's Stortford to Braintree railway line, now an Essex County Council Country Park. Many plants and insects are to be found. Reptiles may be seen basking on the sunny banks and deer also make use of this green corridor.

8. LANGDON NATURE RESERVE
    (Exp 175, GR 659 874)

The Dunton Plotlands is a large remnant of the former south Essex plotlands. Now overgrown, the area is full of wildlife. Many birds use the scrubby woodland to nest in and open areas are good for butterflies. A nearby recreation ground supports an amazing display of several thousand *green-winged orchids*.

9. MALDON WICK
(Exp 183, GR 842 057)

A two-and-a-half kilometre stretch of the former Maldon to Woodham Ferrers railway line, now comprising an Essex Wildlife Trust nature reserve. Many wildflowers grow along the embankment, including *St John's-wort*, *primrose* and *scabious*. The Wick is known for its butterflies, with *green and white-letter hairstreaks* among the twenty-eight recorded.

10. PRIORY PARK
(Exp 175, GR 877 873)

A large park close to Southend town centre set in the grounds of a medieval priory. Many common birds find relative peace and quiet here in spite of its many visitors, but more unusual records include *little egret*, *grey wagtail* and *spotted flycatcher*.

11. RAYLEIGH MOUNT
(Exp 175, GR 804 909)

Ancient castle earthworks now partially wooded. A number of the more common species of butterfly occur, as do the birds, although less common species have included *bullfinch* and passage *pied flycatcher*. Early risers may catch sight of *foxes*.

12. STOW MARIES HALT
(Exp 183, GR 835 991)

A small Essex Wildlife Trust reserve, comprising a short section of the old Maldon to Woodham Ferrers railway line and an area of grassland. Various ferns, including *wall rue* and *black spleenwort* grow on the railway bridge. On the cutting floor, *lizards* scurry among the vegetation, where various wildflowers grow among the thorn scrub. Of the butterflies the *white-letter hairstreak* is notable. Further interest is found in the adjacent grassland where the flora includes *common spotted orchid* and *adders-tongue fern*.

Bibliography

Brooks, S. (1997) *Field Guide to the Dragonflies and Damselflies of Great Britain and Ireland.* Hook: British Wildlife Publishing.

Campbell, A.C. (1976) *The Seashore and Shallow Seas of Britain and Europe.* London: Hamlyn.

Corke, D. *The Nature of Essex.* Buckingham: Barracuda Books.

Dobson, J (1999) The Mammals of Essex. Wimbish: Lopinga Books.

Dowdeswell, W.H. (1984) *Ecology Principles and Practice.* Oxford: Heinemann Educational.

Emmet, A, M. and Heath, J. (eds) (1990) *The Butterflies of Great Britain and Ireland.* Colchester: Harley Books. Emmet, A, M. and Heath, J. (eds) (1990) The Butterflies of Great Britain and Ireland. Colchester: Harley Books.

Essex County Council (1991) *The Essex Environment.* Chelmsford: Essex County Council.

Garrard, I. and Streeter, D. (1998) *The Wild Flowers of the British Isles.* London: Midsummer Books.

Goater, B (1986) *British Pyralid Moths: A Guide to their Identification.* Colchester: Harley Books.

Gunton, T. (2000) *Wild Essex.* Wimbish: Lopinga Books.

Hallet, J. (1995) *Britain in the Wild.* London: Weidenfield and Nicolson.

Jermyn, S. T. (1974) *Flora of Essex.* Colchester: Essex Wildlife Trust.

MacDonald, D. and Barret, P. (1993) *Mammals of Britain and Europe.* London: Collins.

Marshall, J. A. and Haes, C. M. (1990) *Grasshoppers and Allied Insects of Great Britain and Ireland.* Colchester: Harley Books

Morris, P. (ed) (1979) *The Natural History of the British Isles.* Richmond upon Thames: Country Life Books.

Rackham, O. (1986) *The Woods of South-east Essex.* Rochford: Rochford District Council.

Rackham, O. (1994) *The Illustrated History of the Countryside.* London: Seven Dials, Caswell & Co.

Rose, F. (1981) *The Wild Flower Key.* Penguin: London.

Skinner, B. (1998) *Moths of the British Isles.* London: Viking.

Sutherland,W.J. and Hill D.A. (eds) (1995) Managing Habitats for Conservation. Cambridge: Cambridge University Press.

VERTEBRATES

BIRDS

Auks (Alcidae)
Avocet (Recurvirostra, avosetta)
Blackbird (Turdus merula)
Blackcap (Sylvia atricapilla)
Brambling (Fringilla montifringilla)
Bullfinch (Pyrrhula pyrrhula)
Bunting, Corn (Miliaria calandra)
Bunting, Reed (Emberiza schoeniclus)
Buzzard (Buteo buteo)
Chaffinch (Fringilla coelebs)
Chiff Chaff (Phylloscopus collybita)
Coot (Fulica atra)
Cormorant (Phalacrocorax, carbo)
Curlew (Numenius arquata)
Divers (Gavia species)
Duck, Tufted (Aythya fuligula)
Dunlin (Calidris alpina)
Dunnock (Prunella modularis)
Fieldfare (Turdus pilaris)
Flycatcher, Pied (Ficedula hypoleuca)
Gadwall (Anas strepera)
Godwit, Black-tailed (Limosa limosa)
Goldcrest (Regulus regulus)
Golden Plover (Pluvialis apricaria)
Goldeneye (Bucephala clangula)
Goosander (Mergus merganser)
Goose, Brent (Branta bernicula)
Goose, Canada (Branta canadensis)
Grebe, Black-necked (Podiceps grisegena)
Grebe, Great Crested (Podiceps cristatus)
Grebe, Little (Tachybaptus ruficollis)
Grebe, Slavonian (Podiceps auritus)
Gull, Black-headed (Larus ridibundus)
Gull, Common (Larus canus)
Gull, Herring (Larus argentatus)
Gull, Lesser Black-backed (Larus fuscus)
Harrier, Hen (Circus cyaneus)
Harrier, Marsh (Circus aeruginosus)
Hawfinch (Coccothraustes coccothraustes)
Heron, Grey (Ardea cinerea)
Jay (Garrulus glandarius)
Kestrel (Falco tinnunculus)
Kingfisher (Alcedo atthis)
Knot (Calidris canutus)
Lapwing (Vanellus vanellus)
Mallard (Anas platyrhynchos)
Merganser, Red-breasted (Mergus serrator)
Moorhen (Gallinula chloropus)

Nightingale (Luscinia megarhynchos)
Nuthatch (Sitta europea)
Owl, Barn (Tyto alba)
Owl, Little (Athene noctua)
Owl, Short-eared (Asio flammeus)
Owl, Tawny (Strix aluco)
Oystercatcher (Haematopus ostralegus)
Partridge, Grey (Perdix perdix)
Pintail (Anas acuta)
Pipit, Meadow (Anthus pratensis)
Pipit, Tree (Anthus trivialis)
Plover, Ringed (Charadrius hiaticula)
Pochard (Aythya farina)
Redpoll (Carduelis flammea)
Redshank (Tringa tetanus)
Redshank, Spotted (Tringa erythropus)
Redstart (Phoenicurus phoenicurus)
Redwing (Turdus iliacus)
Robin (Erithacus rubecula)
Rook (Corvus frugilegus)
Ruff (Philomachus pugnax)
Sandpiper, Common (Acitis hypoleucos)
Sandpiper, Curlew (Calidris ferruginea)
Sandpiper, Green (Tringa ochropus)
Sandpiper, Wood (Tringa glareola)
Scoter, Common (Melanitta nigra)
Shelduck (Tadorna tadorna)
Shoveler (Anas clypeata)
Siskin (Carduelis spinus)
Skuas (Stercorarius species)
Skylark (Alauda arvensis)
Smew (Mergellus albellus)
Snipe (Gallinago gallinago)
Sparrow, Tree (Passer montanus)
Sparrowhawk (Accipiter nisus)
Starling (Sturnus vulgaris)
Stint, Little (Calidris minuta)
Swallow (Hirundo rustica)
Swan, Mute (Cygnus olor)
Swift (Apus apus)
Teal (Anas crecca)
Tern, Common (Sterna hirundo)
Tern, Little (Sterna albifrons)
Thrush, Mistle (Turdus viscivorus)
Tit, Bearded (Panurus biarmicus)
Tit, Blue (Parus caeruleus)
Tit, Coal (Parus ater)
Tit, Marsh (Parus palustris)
Tit, Willow (Parus montanus)
Treecreeper (Certhia familiaris)
Wagtail, Grey (Motacilla cinerea)

Wagtail, Pied (Motacilla alba)
Wagtail, Yellow (Motacilla flava)
Warbler, Cetti's (Cettia cetti)
Warbler, Garden (Sylvia borin)
Warbler, Grasshopper (Locustella naevia)
Warbler, Reed (Acrocephalus scirpaceus)
Warbler, Sedge (Acrocephalus
    schoenobeanus)
Warbler, Willow (Pylloscopus, trochilus)
Whimbrel (Numenius phaeopus)
Whitethroat (Sylvia communis)
Whitethroat, Lesser (Sylvia curruca)
Wigeon (Anas Penelope)
Woodpecker, Great Spotted (Dendrocopos
    major)
Woodpecker, Green (Picus viridis)
Woodpecker, Lesser Spotted (Dendrocopos
    minor)
Yellowhammer (Emberiza citrinella)

MAMMALS
Badger (Meles meles)
Bat, Brown long-eared (Plecotus auritus)
Bat, Daubenton's (Myotis daubentonii)
Bat, Noctule (Nyctalus noctula)
Deer, Fallow (Dama dama)
Deer, Red (Cervus elaphus)
Deer, Roe (Capreolus capreolus)
Dormouse (Muscardinus avellanarius)
Fox, Red (Vulpes vulpes)
Hare, Brown (Lepus europaeus)
Hedgehog (Erinaceus europaeus)
Mouse, Harvest (Micromys minutus)
Mouse, Wood (Apodemus sylvaticus)
Mouse, Yellow-necked (Apodemus
    flavicollis)
Muntjac (Muntiacus reevsi)
Otter (Lutra lutra)
Pipistrelle (Pipistrellus pipistrellus)
Rabbit (Oryctolagus cuniculus)
Shrew, Common (Sorex araneus)
Shrew, Water (Neomys fodiens)
Squirrel, Grey (Sciurus carolinensis)
Stoat (Mustela emrinea)
Vole, Bank (Clethrionomys glareolus)
Vole, Field (Microtus agrestis)
Vole, Water (Arvicola terrestris)
Weasel (Mustela nivalis)

REPTILES AND AMPHIBIANS
Adder (Vipera berus)

Frog, Common (Rana temporaria)
Frog, Marsh (Rana ridibunda)
Lizard, Common (Lacerta vivipara
Newt, Great-crested (Triturus cristatus)
Newt, Palmate (Triturus Helvetica)
Newt, Smooth (Triturus vulgaris)
Snake, Grass (Natrix natrix)
Toad, Common (Bufo bufo)

FISH
Chub (Leucusus cephalus)
Gudgeon (Gobio gobio)
Perch (Perca fluviatilis)
Pike (Esox lucius)
Roach (Rutilis rutilis)
Rudd (Scardinius erythrophthalmus)

INVERTEBRATES

INSECTS
Springtails (Collembolla)

MAYFLIES (EPHEMEROPTERA)
Mayfly (Ephemera danica)

DRAGONFLIES AND DAMSELFLIES
    (ODONATA)
Chaser, Broad-bodied (Libellula depressa)
Chaser, Scarce (Libellula fulva)
Damselfly, Azure (Coenagrion puella)
Damselfly, Common Blue (Enallagma
    cyathigerum)
Damselfly, Emerald (Lestes sponsa)
Damselfly, Large Red (Pyrrhosoma
    nymphula)
Damselfly, Scarce Emerald (Lestes dryas)
Darter, Common (Sympetrum striolatum)
Darter, Ruddy (Sympetrum sanguineum)
Demoiselle, Banded (Calopteryx splendens)
Demoiselle, Beautiful (Calopteryx virgo)
Dragonfly, Emperor (Anax imperator)
Emerald, Downy (Cordulia aenea)
Hawker, Brown (Aeshna grandis)
Hawker, Migrant (Aeshna mixta)
Hawker, Southern (Aeshna cyanea)

GRASSHOPPERS AND CRICKETS
    (ORTHOPTERA)
Bush-cricket, Dark (Pholidoptera
    griseoaptera)
Bush-cricket, Oak (Meconema thalissinum)

Bush-cricket, Roesel's (Metrioptera roeselii)

Bush-cricket, Speckled (Leptophyes punctatissima)

Conehead, Short-winged (Conocephalus dorsalis)

Grasshopper, Field (Chorthippus brunneus)

Grasshopper, Lesser Marsh (C. albomarginatus)

Grasshopper, Meadow (Chorthippus parallelus)

Groundhopper, Common (Tetrix undulata)

BUGS (HEMIPTERA)

Bug (Notostira elongata)

Bug (Stenodema laevigatum)

Flower Bug, Common (Anthocoris nemorum)

Froghopper, Red and Black (Cercopis vulnerata)

Froghoppers (Aphrophoridae family)

Pond Skater (Gerris lacustris)

Water Cricket (Velia caprai)

Water Measurer (Hydrometra stagnorum)

Water Scorpion (Nepa cinerea)

Water Stick Insect (Ranatra linearis)

Water boatman or Backswimmer Notonecta glauca)

Water boatman, Lesser (Corixa species)

BUTTERFLIES AND MOTHS (LEPIDOPTERA)

Admiral, White (Limenitis camilla)

Argus, Brown (Aricia agestis)

Blue, Common (Polyommatus icarus)

Blue, Holly (Celastrina argiolus)

Brimstone (Gonepteryx rhamni)

Brown, Meadow (Maniola jurtina)

Comma (Polygonia c-album)

Fritillary, Heath (Mellicta athalia)

Gatekeeper (Pyronia tithonus)

Hairstreak, Green (Callophrys rubi)

Hairstreak, Purple (Quercusia quercus)

Hairstreak, White-letter (Strymonidia w-album)

Heath, Small (Coenonympha pamphilus)

Orange Tip (Anthocharis cardamines)

Ringlet (Aphantopus hyperantus)

Skipper, Essex (Thymelicus flavus)

Skipper, Large (Ochlodes venatus)

Skipper, Small (Thymelicus lineola)

Speckled Wood (Pararge aegeria)

White, Marbled (Melanargia galathea)

White, Small (Artogea rapea)

Brimstone (Opisthograptis luteolata)

Burnet Companion (Euclidia glyphica)

Burnet, Six-spot (Zyaena filipendulae)

Carpet, Chalk (Scotopteryx bipunctaria)

China-mark, Small (Cataclysta lemnata)

Emperor Moth (Saturnia pavonia)

Fisher's Estuarine Moth (Gortyna borelii lunata)

Footman, Common (Eilema lurideola)

Footman, Scarce (Eilema complana)

Hawk-moth, Elephant (Deilephila elpenor)

Heath, Latticed (Semiothisa clathrata)

Hook-tip, Oak (Drepana falcataria)

Longhorn, Degeer's (Nemophora degeerella)

Longhorn, Green (Adela reaumurella)

Thorn, Purple (Selenia tetralunaria)

Tiger, Cream-spot (Arctia villica)

Tortrix, Green Oak (Tortrix viridana)

Underwing, Orange (Archiearis parthenias)

Wave, Common White (Cabera pusaria)

CADDIS FLIES (TRICHOPTERA)

TRUE FLIES (DIPTERA)

Hoverflies (Syrphidae family)

Leatherjackets / Cranefly larvae (Tipulidae)

ANTS, WASPS, BEES AND KIN (HYMENOPTERA)

Ant, Wood (Formica rufa)

Bumblebees (Bombus family)

Carder Bee, Shrill (Bombus sylvarum)

Gall Wasp, Spangle (Neuroterus quercus-baccarum)

BEETLES (COLEOPTERA)

Beetle (Oedemera nobilis)

Beetle, Great Diving (Dytiscus marginalis)

Beetle, Sailor (Cantharis rustica)

Beetle, Soldier (Rhagonycha fulva)

Beetle, Whirlygig (Gyrinus natator)

Longhorn Beetle (Strangalia maculata)

Water Beetle (Ilybius species)

SPIDERS

Sheet-web Spider (Agelena labyrinthica)

Tetragnetha extensa

Wasp Spider (Argiope bruennichi)
Wolf Spider (Pardosa lugubris)

MOLLUSCS

Cockle, Common (Cerastoderma edule)
Laver Spire Shell (Hydrobia ulvae)
Limpet, Slipper (Crepidula fornicata)
Mussel (Mytilus edulis)
Peppery Furrow Shell (Scrobicularia plana)
Periwinkle, Common (Littorina littorea)
Sand Gaper (Mya aranaria)
Snail, Amber (Succinea putris)
Snail, Pond (Lymnaea stagnalis)
Snail, Ramshorn (Planorbis species)
Tellin, Baltic (Macoma balthica)

CRUSTACEANS

Corophium volutator
Sandhopper (Talitrus saltator)
Sea-slater (Ligia oceanica)
Shrimp, Common (Crangon vulgaris)
Shrimp, Freshwater (Gammarus pulex)
Water-flea (Cyclops)
Water-flea (Daphnia)
Waterlouse (Asellus aquaticus)

OTHER INVERTEBRATES

Sea Urchin (Psammechinus miliaris)
Beadlet Anemone (Actinia equina)
Ragworm (Nereis diversicolor)
Lugworm (Arenicola marina)

FLORA

VASCULAR PLANTS

Agrimony (Agrimonia eupatoria)
Alder (Alnus glutinosa)
Archangel, Yellow (Lamiastrum galeobdolon
Ash (Fraxinus excelsior)
Aster, Sea (Aster tripolium)
Avens, Wood (Geum urbanum)
Barley, Wood (Hordelymus europaeus)
Bartsia, Red (Odontites vernus)
Bedstraw, Marsh (Galium palustre)
Beech (Fagus sylvaticus)
Bent, Creeping (Agrostis stolonifera)
Birch (Betula pendula and pubescens)
Blackthorn (Prunus spinosa)
Bluebell (Hyacinthoides non-scripta)

Broom (Cytisus scoparia)
Bugle (Ajuga reptans)
Bulrush (Scirpus lacustris)
Buttercup, Meadow (Ranunculus acris)
Campion, Red (Silene dioica)
Carrot, Wild (Daucas carota)
Chestnut, Horse (Aesculus hippocastanum)
Chestnut, Sweet (Castanea sativa)
Chicory (Cichorium intybus)
Clover, Sea (Trifolium squamosum)
Clover, Sulphur (Trifolium ochroleucon)
Cock's-foot (Dactylis glomerata)
Cord-grass (Spartina species)
Corncockle (Agrostemma githago)
Cornflower (Centaurea cyanus)
Cowslip (Primula veris)
Cow-wheat, Common (Melampyrum pratense)
Cranesbill, Dove's-foot (Geranium molle)
Cuckooflower (Cardamine pratensis)
Daisy, Ox-eye (Leucanthemum vulgare)
Dog's-tail, Crested (Cynosurus cristatus)
Fennel, Hog's (Peucedanum officinale)
Fern, Adder's tongue (Ophioglossum vulgatum)
Fescue, Red (Festuca rubra)
Fescue, Sheep's (Festuca ovina)
Forget-me-not, Water (Myosotis scorpioides)
Foxglove (Digitalis purpurea)
Foxtail, Meadow (Alopecrus geniculatus)
Gentian, Autumn (Gentianella amarella)
Glasswort (Salicornia species)
Gorse (Ulex europaeus)
Grass, Eel (Zostera species)
Grass, Sweet Vernal (Anthoxanthum odoratum)
Hair-grass, Early (Aira praecox)
Hair-grass, Tufted (Deschampsia caespitosa)
Hawthorn (Crataegus monogyna)
Hazel (Corylus avellana)
Heath, Cross-leaved (Erica tetralix)
Heather, Bell (Erica cinerea)
Hedge-parsley, Knotted (Torilis nodosa)
Helleborine, Broad-leaved (Epipactis helleborine)
Hemp-agrimony (Eupatorium cannabinum)
Herb Robert (Geranium robertianum)
Herb-paris (Paris quadrifolia)
Hogweed (Heracleum sphondylium)

Holly (Ilex aquifolium)
Honeysuckle (Lonicera periclymenum)
Hornbeam (Carpinus betulus)
Iris, Yellow (Iris psuedacorus)
Ivy (Hedera helix)
Knapweed, Lesser (Centaurea nigra)
Lily of the Valley (Convallaria majalis)
Lime, Small-leaved (Tilia cordata
Ling (Calluna vulgaris)
Loosestrife, Purple (Lythrum salicaria)
Maple, Field (Acer campestre)
Meadow-grass, Rough (Poa trivialis)
Meadowsweet (Filipendula ulmaria)
Medick, Black (Medicago lupulina)
Melick, Wood (Melica uniflora)
Milkwort, Heath (Polygala serpyllifolia)
Mint, Water (Mentha aquatica)
Moschatel (Adoxa moschatellina)
Nettle, Stinging (Urtica dioica)
Nightshade, Deadly (Atropa belladonna)
Nightshade, Enchanter's (Circaea lutetiana)
Oak (Quercus robur and petrea)
Orchid, Bee (Ophrys apifera)
Orchid, Common Spotted (Dactylorhiza
    fuchsii)
Orchid, Early Purple (Orchis mascula)
Orchid, Greater Butterfly (Platanthera
    chlorantha)
Orchid, Green-winged (Orchis morio)
Orchid, Pyramidal (Anacamptis
    pyramidalis)
Orchid, Southern Marsh (Dactylorhiza
    praetermissa)
Oxlip (Primula elatior)
Ox-tongue, Bristly (Picris echioides)
Parsley, Cow (Anthriscus sylvestris)
Plane, London (Platanus x hispanica)
Plantain, Ribwort (Plantago lanceolata)
Pondweed, Broad-leaved (Potamogeton
    natans)
Pondweed, Fennel (Potamogeton
    pectinatus)
Poppy, Yellow-horned (Glaucium flavum)
Primrose (Primula vulgaris)
Purslane, Sea (Atriplex portulacoides)
Rattle, Yellow (Rhinanthus minor)
Reed, Common (Phragmites communis)
Reedmace (Typha)
Rush, Soft (Juncus effusus)
Salad Burnet (Sanguisorba minor)
Samphire, Golden (Inula crithmoides)

Scabious, Field (Knautia arvensis)
Sea-holly (Erngium maritimum)
Sea-lavender (Limonium vulgare)
Sedge, Green-ribbed (Carex binervis)
Sedge, Pendulous (Carex pendula)
Sedge, Pill (Carex pilulifera)
Self-heal (Prunella vulgaris)
Sorrel, Common (Rumex acetosa)
Spearwort, Lesser (Ranunculus flammula)
Spleenwort, Black (Asplenium adiantum)
Spleenwort, Maidenhair (Asplenium
    trichomanes)
Spruce, Sitka (Picea sitchensis)
St John's-wort (Hypericum species)
Stitchwort, Greater (Stellaria holostea)
Stonecrop, Biting (Sedum acre)
Trefoil, Bird's-foot (Lotus corniculatus)
Trefoil, Narrow-leaved Bird's-foot
    (Lotus glaber)
Twayblade (Listera ovata)
Vetch, Kidney (Anthyllis vulneraria)
Vetchling, Grass (Lathyrus nissolia)
Vetchling, Meadow (Lathyrus pratensis)
Wall Rue (Asplenium ruta-muraria)
Water-crowfoot (Ranunculus aquatilis)
Water-lily, Yellow (Nuphar lutea)
Water-plantain (Alisma plantago-aquatica)
Water-violet (Hottonia palustris)
Willow (Salix)
Willowherb, Rosebay (Chamerion
    angustifolium)
Wintergreen, Round-leaved (Pyrola
    rotundifolia)
Woodrush, Great Hairy (Luzula sylvatica)
Woundwort, Hedge (Stachy sylvatica)
Yew (Taxus bacata)
Yorkshire Fog (Holcus lanatus)

ALGAE
Wrack, Bladder (Fuscus vesiculosus)
Wrack, Knotted (Ascophyllum nodosum)

FUNGI
Bolete (Boletus species)
Death Cap (Amanita phalloides)
Ink Cap, Magpie (Coprinus picaceus)
Milkcap (Lactarius species)
Panther Cap (Amanita pantherina)
Polypore, Many-zoned (Coriolus versicolor)
Russula (Russula species)
Sulphur Tuft (Hypholoma fasciculare)